Family Guide to Assistive Technology

Family Guide to Assistive Technology

Written and edited by

Katharin A. Kelker, Ed.D.

&

Roger Holt

BROOK
L I N E
BOOKS

Brookline Books
Cambridge, Massachusetts

Co-published with The Federation For Children with Special Needs, Boston

ISBN 1-57129-074-5

Library of Congress Cataloging-in-Publication Data
Kelker, Katharin A.
    Family guide to assistive technology / written and edited by Katharin A. Kelker, Roger Holt ; [illustration by Karen Moss]
    p. cm.
    ISBN 1-57129-074-5 (alk. paper)
    1. Self-help devices for the disabled. 2. Rehabilitation. I. Holt, Roger.
II. Federation for Children with Special Needs. III. Title.
RM698 .K45 1999
618.92'003--dc21   99-0446711

This material is available upon request in alternative formats by calling 1-800-222-7585.

Published by
Brookline Books
P.O Box 381047
Cambridge MA 02238-1047
Order Toll Free : 1-800-666-BOOK

in collaboration with
The Federation for Children with Special Needs
1135 Tremont St, Suite 420
Boston, MA 02120

CONTENTS

INTRODUCTION

Assistive technology is redefining what is possible for people with a wide range of cognitive and physical disabilities. In the home, classroom, workplace, and community, assistive technology is enabling individuals with disabilities to be more independent, self-confident, productive, and better integrated into the mainstream.

Beginning early in life, technology is making it possible for children with disabilities to do more for themselves. A child who cannot use her hands can operate a computer with a switch and an on-screen keyboard. A child who cannot speak can communicate using a portable electronic device that speaks. A child who is unable to get in and out of the bathtub can be safely and easily lifted using a mechanical device. These are just a few examples of the wide variety of equipment, called assistive technology, that is available today.

Assistive technology can mean anything from simple, homemade devices to highly sophisticated environmental control systems. It can be adapted toys, computers, powered mobility, augmentative communication devices, special switches, and thousands of commercially available or adapted tools to assist an individual with learning, working, and interacting socially.

As wonderful as assistive technology can be, it is not always easy to acquire. It takes expertise and persistence to find the correct devices and figure out ways to pay for them. For example, children with disabilities who are eligible for special education have a legal right to technology to assist them with learning. Both the Individualized Family Service Plan (IFSP) and the Individualized Education Program (IEP) which are required by the Individuals with Disabilities Education Act (IDEA) are potentially powerful tools for incorporating assistive technology into the education of students with disabilities. But assistive technology does not become part of a student's special education plan unless parents are knowledgeable about technology and know what to do to ensure that assistive technology becomes an integral part of their child's program.

This *Guide* is intended to help parents learn more about assistive technology and how it can help their children. The *Guide* includes tips for getting started, ideas about where to look for money, and suggestions for what to do when applying for funding. Places to contact for more information or to find software and equipment are listed in the Appendix at the end of the *Guide*.

Finding and paying for the right technology requires commitment and energy. Professionals in education and medicine should help. As a parent, you have a much better chance of getting what is needed if you and your child are involved in selecting the technology and planning for its use. This *Guide* should help you to understand the processes for acquiring assistive technology and provide you with the tools to advocate for your child's special technology needs.

— *The Authors*

CHAPTER 1

Defining Assistive Technology

Assistive technology devices are aids which substitute for or enhance the function of some physical or mental ability. Assistive technology can be anything homemade, purchased off the shelf modified, or commercially available which is used to help an individual perform some task of daily living. The term *assistive technology* encompasses a broad range of devices from "low tech" (e.g., pencil grips, splints, paper stabilizers) to "high tech" (e.g., computers, voice synthesizers, braille readers). These devices include the entire range of supportive tools and equipment from adapted spoons to wheelchairs and computer systems for environmental control.

The Individuals with Disabilities Education Act (IDEA), the federal special education law, provides the following legal definition of an *assistive technology device:* "any item, piece of equipment, or product system ... that is used to increase, maintain, or improve functional capabilities of individuals with disabilities." Under IDEA, assistive technology devices can be used in the educational setting to provide a variety of accommodations or adaptations for people with disabilities.

The IDEA also lists the services a school district may need to provide in order to ensure that assistive technology is useful to a student in the school setting. The law defines *assistive technology service* as: "**any service that directly assists an individual with a** disability in the selection, acquisition, or use of an assistive technology device." This service includes all of the following possibilities:

- evaluation of the technology needs of the individual, including a functional evaluation in the individual's customary environment;

- purchasing, leasing, or otherwise providing for the acquisition of assistive technology devices for individuals with disabilities;

- selecting, designing, fitting, customizing, adapting, applying, maintaining, repairing, or replacing of assistive technology devices;

- coordinating and using other therapies, interventions, or services with assistive technology devices, such as those associated with existing education and rehabilitation plans and programs;

- assistive technology training or technical assistance with assistive technology for an individual with a disability, or, where appropriate, the family of an individual with disabilities;

- training or technical assistance for professionals, employers, or other individuals who provide services to, employ, or otherwise are substantially involved in the major life functions of individuals with disabilities.

The intention of the special education law is that, if a student with disabilities needs technology in order to be able to learn, the school district will (a) evaluate the student's technology needs, (b) acquire the necessary technology, (c) coordinate technology use with other therapies and interventions, and (d) provide training for the individual, the individual's family, and the school staff in the effective use of the technology.

During the time that students with disabilities are in school, they can have the opportunity to learn to use technology at the same time they are learning academic subjects and social skills. The efficient and effective use of assistive technology can be as basic a skill for students with disabilities as reading, writing, and arithmetic since the use of technology can go a long way toward circumventing the limitations imposed by the disability and provide these students with a "level playing field" in every area of life accomplishment.

What is an accommodation?

Accommodations are reasonable modifications that are made to compensate for skills or abilities that an individual lacks. For example, if a person does not digest spicy foods well, we might accommodate this individual by adjusting the diet so that the person was eating only bland foods. When the word *accommodation* is used in connection with disability issues, it refers to a way of modifying a task or assignment so that a person with a disability can participate in spite of whatever challenges the disability may pose. For example, when a student who is unable to remember math facts is allowed to do math problems with a calculator, the use of the calculator is an accommodation which allows the student to work around his disability. With an accommodation, the student can still perform math problems, but the student does so using a different method.

In the school setting, sometimes it is necessary to make accommodations for individuals with disabilities in order to compensate for skills or abilities, they do not have. For example, for some students with learning disabilities, it may be necessary to encourage the student to use alternative methods for spelling like a spell check software program on the computer or a hand-held spelling device.

What is an adaptation? How does adaptation differ from accommodation?

Adaptation means developing unique devices or methods designed specifically to assist persons with disabilities to perform daily tasks.

An adaptation is something specially designed which is not normally used by other people. An *accommodation*, on the other hand, is simply a change in routine, method, or approach which may be used by people with or without disabilities. Examples of adaptations include special grips to turn stove knobs or specially designed keyboards to operate computers. (Two books by Doreen Greenstein, *Backyards and Butterflies* (1995) and *Easy Things to Make ... To Make Things Easy* (1997), published by Brookline Books, describe both accommodations and useful adaptations for children and adults with disabilities).

What are common types of assistive technology? Does assistive technology just mean computers?

Assistive technology certainly includes computers, but it also refers to a number of other types of accommodations and adaptations which enable individuals with disabilities to function more independently. Computers are an important type of assistive technology because they open up so many exciting possibilities for writing, speaking, finding information, or controlling an individual's environment. But computers are not the only avenues to solving problems through technology. There are many low-tech (and low-cost) solutions for problems that disabilities pose. Examples of inexpensive, low-tech solutions include wrist splints, clip boards for holding papers steady, or Velcro tabs to keep positioning pads in place.

The following is a list of common assistive technology applications:

Positioning. In the classroom, students with physical disabilities may need assistance with their sitting positions so they can participate effectively in school work. Generally, therapists try to achieve an upright, forward facing position by using padding, structured chairs, straps, supports, or restraints to hold the body in a stable and comfortable manner. Also considered is the student's position in relation to peers and the teacher. Often, it is necessary to design positioning systems for a variety of settings so that the student can participate in multiple activities at school. Examples of equipment used for positioning are side lying frames, walkers, crawling assists, floor sitters, chair inserts, wheelchairs, straps, trays, standing aids, bean bag chairs, sand bags and so forth.

Access. To participate in school tasks, some students require special devices to access computers or environmental controls. The first step in providing access is to determine which body parts can be used to indicate the student's intentions. Controllable, anatomical sites like eyes, the head, neck, or mouth movements may have sufficient movement to operate equipment which will allow access to the computer. Once a controllable, anatomical site has been identified, then decisions can be made about input devices, selec-

Figure 1: Alternative and Processing Computer Access Methods

Input	Processing	Output
Alternate keyboards	Abbreviation/expansion and macro programs	Braille displays and embossers
Interface devices		Monitor additions
Joysticks	Access utilities	Screen enlargement programs
Keyboard modifications	Menu management programs	
Keyboard additions		Screen readers
Optical pointing devices	Reading comprehension programs	Speech synthesizers
Pointing and typing aids		Talking and large print word processors
Switches with scanning	Writing composition programs	
Scanners & optical character recognition	Writing enhancement tools (e.g. grammar checkers)	
Trackballs		
Touch screens		
Voice recognition		

tion techniques (direct, scanning), and acceleration strategies (coding, prediction). Input devices include such things as switches, alternative keyboards, mice, trackballs, touch windows, speech recognition software, and head pointers. Once computer access has been established, it should be coordinated with other systems the student is using, including powered mobility, communication or listening devices, and environmental control systems.

Access can also refer to physical entrance and exit of buildings or facilities. This kind of assistive technology includes modifications to buildings, rooms and other facilities, such as ramps, door openers, braille directions, and location and position of pay phones, and elevator controls to allow access and freedom of movement of people with disabilities. Accessibility to shopping centers, places of business, schools, recreation and transportation is possible because of assistive technology modifications.

Environmental Control. Independent use of equipment in the classroom can be achieved for students with physical disabilities through various types of environmental controls including remote controls switches, and special adaptations of on/off switches, to make them accessible (e.g. velcro attachments, pointer sticks). Robotic arms and other environmental control systems turn lights on and off, open doors, operate appliances. Locational and orientation systems give people with vision impairments information about where they are, what the ground nearby is like, and whether or not there is a curb close by.

Augmentative Communication. Every student in school needs to communicate in order to interact with others and learn from social contact. Students who cannot speak or whose speech is difficult for others to understand may benefit from using some type of communication device or devices. Communication devices include such things as symbol systems, communication boards and wallets, programmable switches, electronic communication devices, speech synthesizers, recorded speech devices, communication enhancement software, and voiced word processing.

Assistive Listening. Much of the time in school, students are expected to learn through listening. Students who have difficulty with hearing or auditory processing can be at a distinct disadvantage unless they learn to use the hearing they have, or they develop alternative means for getting information. Whether hearing problems are progressive, permanent, or intermittent, they may interfere significantly with learning to speak, read, and follow directions. Assistive devices to help with hearing and auditory processing problems include: hearing aids, personal FM units, sound field FM systems, Phonic Ear, TDDs, or closed caption TV.

Visual Aids. Vision is also a major learning mode. General methods for assisting with vision problems include increasing contrast, enlarging stimuli and making use of tactile and auditory models. Devices that assist with vision include screen readers, screen enlargers, magnifiers, large-type books, taped books, Braillers, light boxes, high contrast materials, thermoform graphics, synthesizers, and scanners.

Mobility. Any number of devices may assist students in getting around the school building and participating in student activities. Mobility devices include such things as self-propelled walkers, manual or powered wheelchairs, and powered recreational vehicles like bikes and scooters.

Social Interaction and Recreation. Students with disabilities want to have fun and interact socially with their peers. Assistive technology can help them to participate in all sorts of recreational activities. Some adapted recreational activities include drawing software, computer games, computer simulations, painting with a head or mouth wand, interactive laser disks, and adapted puzzles. Adaptations can also be made closer to the usual activities and games; e.g., dodgeball can have adapted rules to allow her participation with other students.

Computer-Based Instruction. Computer-based instruction can make possible independent participation in activities related to the curriculum. Software can be selected which mirrors the conceptual framework of the regular curriculum, but offers an alternative way of responding to exercises and learning activities. Software can provide the tools for written expression, spelling, calculation, reading, basic reasoning, and higher level thinking skills. The computer can also be used to access a wide variety of databases.

Self-Care. In order to benefit from education, some students require assistance with self-care activities like feeding, dressing, and toileting. Assistive devices for self-care include such things as robotics, electric feeders, adapted utensils, specially designed toilet seats, and aids for tooth brushing, washing, dressing, and grooming.

What sort of students might use assistive technology?

Students who benefit from assistive technology are those with mental or physical disabilities that interfere with learning or life functions. The technology helps the student to overcome or compensate for the disability and be more independent in participating at school. Students who benefit from assistive technology may have mild learning disabilities or they may have physical or cognitive disabilities that range from mild to severe. Assistive technology is not necessary or helpful for every student in special education, but it is an important part of the support system for many students with identified disabilities.

Isn't assistive technology appropriate only for students with more severe disabilities?

Assistive technology is simply a set of tools that can be used to address some need that a person may have. For individuals with severe mental or physical disabilities, the technological solutions can help to meet multiple and complex needs. But individuals with less complex needs also can benefit from assistive technology. For example, individuals with learning disabilities who have difficulty with reading or writing can benefit educationally from using the word processing and voiced reading capabilities of computers.

Isn't assistive technology just a crutch? Won't students become too dependent on technology and not learn to use the skills they have?

Assistive technology should be used as support for access, learning and performing daily tasks. In general, assistive technology is appropriate when it compensates for disabilities so that the individual can function independently. If assistive technology is necessary for a student to have access to educational opportunities or to benefit from education, then it is not a "crutch," but a legitimate support.

The use of assistive technology enhances function and increases skills and opportunities. Students may need a particular device to perform skillfully, just as many people need glasses to focus. Denying the device denies the student an opportunity to achieve success at the level of his or her potential.

When is using assistive technology appropriate?

Assistive technology may be considered appropriate when it does any or all of the following things:

- Enables an individual to perform functions that can be achieved by no other means.

- Ameliorates the limitations imposed by disability as well as the handicaps imposed by inaccessible environments.

- Provides access for participation in programs or activities which otherwise would be closed to the individual.

- Increases endurance or ability to persevere and complete tasks that otherwise are too laborious to be attempted on a routine basis.

- Enables an individual to concentrate on learning or employment tasks, rather than mechanical tasks.

- Provides greater access to information.

- Supports social interactions with peers and adults.

- Supports participation in the least restrictive educational environment.

SUMMARY

Assistive technology means any device which helps an individual with a disability to perform tasks of daily living and learning. There is a wide range of types of devices from low-tech, homemade aids to computers and sophisticated electronic equipment. Assistive technology is one of the services which can be provided in a special education program under the Individuals with Disabilities Education Act (IDEA). IDEA requires that students who need assistive technology receive the aids and devices and the assistive technology services (e.g., evaluation for assistive technology and modification and maintenance of equipment) they need to benefit from a free, appropriate public education.

KEY POINTS

- Technology can help students get an appropriate education.

- Technology can make the school setting less restrictive.

- Schools must evaluate students and identify technology that will help students.

- The IEP is an important tool for students to get technology.

- Schools must provide technology that allows students to participate in educational activities.

- Students' needs should be reviewed each year, and new technology can be provided by the school as needs change.

HINTS FOR PARENTS

It is never too soon to consider using assistive technology. Some infants with physical disabilities, for example, really benefit from early interaction with toys that operate by a switch. Here are suggestions for times to evaluate a child for assistive technology:

- **When disability limits interaction with the environment and interferes with experiential learning.**

  Assistive technology can be used to provide physical access to the environment (e.g., switch toys, floor scooters, touchwindow).

- **When a need for assistance with expressive language is identified.**

  Assistive technology can assist with expression through the use of programmable switches, electronic communication devices, voiced word processing, braille embossing and so forth.

- **When an individual's motor performance interferes with learning.**

  If handwriting, for example, is very slow and laborious for an individual, and the result is difficult to read, use of a word processing device can provide a truer picture of what the child knows and is able to do, thus allowing fuller participation with peers.

- **When a physical disability is impeding the educational/vocational opportunities open to an individual.**

  Assistive technology can provide access to the workplace, for example, by allowing an individual who is blind to learn to use a screen reader and voiced word processing to do clerical tasks that would otherwise be impossible.

- **When a disability is impeding an individual's independence.**

  Sometimes assistive technology can be used to allow a person with a disability to function more independently. For example, a powered wheelchair allows an individual to travel independently.

A CHILD'S SITUATION TO CONSIDER: SARA

Sara, who has Down syndrome, is eight years old. Her language and speech skills are three years delayed, but she has age appropriate social skills. Sara has spent part of her school day in a regular classroom ever since kindergarten, but this year her third grade teacher is suggesting that Sara really cannot keep up with her classmates. The teacher thinks that Sara would be better off in a self-contained class with students who work at her pace.

Sara needs help with fine motor coordination and she has had difficulty learning to write in cursive. Her oral reading is difficult to understand. However, Sara is good at addition and subtraction, having mastered adding with carrying and subtraction with borrowing. She reads at about a second-grade level with good comprehension. Sara's parents would like to see her continue in the regular classroom for as much time as possible, but they recognize that Sara's writing and speaking present challenges.

- *What are Sara's needs?*

- *What kinds of technology should go in Sara's Individual Education Plan (IEP)?*

- *How would you make a case for putting assistive technology into her IEP?*

Sara's Solution

Sara's IEP Team met and concluded that she is doing well in a regular classroom setting; she is making adequate progress in academic skills and has learned how to interact socially with her peers. However, some simple accommodations and technology may help Sara to work faster and more efficiently.

At this point Sara may need some assistance with handwriting and speaking, but the solutions to her problems in these areas need not be complex ones. The Team decided that Sara should continue to practice cursive until she has mastered all the letters and can be more facile in using script. However, while she is still learning cursive, she needs other means for responding in writing. For short written responses, the team agreed that Sara should be encouraged to use manuscript printing. When speed is important or when writing assignments are longer, Sara should have access to a computer with an adaptive keyboard (e.g., IntelliKeys). The adaptive keyboard is helpful for Sara because the "keys" are larger and easier to see. Using the keyboard requires only a very light touch so Sara finds it easier to use than a standard computer keyboard.

For oral reading, the team decided to have Sara practice reading into a tape recorder. Her speech therapist will work with her on slowing down her rate of speech and reading with expression. When Sara has a good tape of her oral reading, she will submit it to her teacher for review and presentation to her class.

Solution Summary

Practice cursive

Use manuscript printing for short assignments

Use computer with adaptive keyboard for longer assignments

Practice oral reading using a tape recorder

CHAPTER 2

Making Assistive Technology Decisions

When parents learn about assistive technology and the wonderful opportunities it can provide, they often want to jump right in and get the latest in technology for their children. Who wouldn't want an augmentative communication device for a child who cannot talk? What parents wouldn't want to get a computer if it would help their child learn?

When the world of assistive technology opens up for parents, it can be like entering a great toy store—everything looks so wonderful that it makes it hard to know what to select. Choosing the right device to meet an individual child's needs requires technical knowledge and indepth understanding of the child's functional capabilities. Not only is the selection of a device made difficult by the complexity of the equipment and the special needs of the child, assistive technology devices can be very expensive. Making such purchases can be a major financial commitment for school districts and families, one that takes a great deal of fact finding, planning, and sometimes significant sacrifice.

Families invest more than money in their children's assistive technology. Practical investments of time and effort and emotional investments of hope and enthusiasm are made with every assistive technology purchase. Because of the high level of financial, personal and emotional commitment, family disappointment is great when equipment fails to perform as expected.

Buying and then not using a device because of dissatisfaction can be a devastating experience for all concerned. That is why it is so important for parents and schools to proceed cautiously into the world of assistive technology and make purchases only after careful evaluation and trials with the new device. Following is a summary of suggestions to consider before making any assistive technology purchase: be realistic about the child's capabilities and needs; get a multidisciplinary evaluation; examine available technology with a critical eye; match the child's needs to specific equipment features; do not make a purchase until you have used the device for a trial period; identify next steps; and determine what needs to be done for follow-up after purchase.

GUIDELINES FOR MAKING ASSISTIVE TECHNOLOGY DECISIONS

Be realistic about your child's capabilities and needs.

Assistive technology can open up exciting new opportunities for a child, but it is not magic. There are certain basic requirements for any individual to be successful with technology, and it is important to face these requirements squarely. There is nothing more disappointing or discouraging than purchasing expensive equipment for a child which she is unable to use.

Prerequisites for Computer Use. The child must be able to understand that the computer operates (e.g., changes, does something) because the child has activated the equipment through some volitional movement or activity (e.g., eyebeam, speaking, puffing into a straw, hitting a switch). Some children enjoy playing with switches by hitting them randomly but may not yet be able to connect their own behavior to the response their movement activates. In order to be successful in interacting with a computer, the user must be able to control some activity and to do so consistently. For example, the child would have to be able to activate the computer in response to a visual, tactile, or auditory prompt.

Another prerequisite to computer use is the ability to make conscious, meaningful choices between alternatives like *yes* and *no*. The choices can be very simple ones, but there has to be evidence that the child has made an actual decision and not merely acted randomly. Learning how to make such choices may be a necessary goal on the child's Individual Educational Plan (IEP).

If a child cannot learn the concept of cause and effect or cannot learn to make consistent choices, using a computer is probably not a worthwhile next step at this point in the child's development. Other types of activities may be more appropriate, less expensive, and just as rewarding developmentally and personally.

Prerequisites for Augmentative Communication. These communication devices can literally give voice to the thoughts of individuals who cannot speak or cannot speak clearly, so they are understood but—again—these devices are not magic. Electronic communication devices are of no value unless the user has some *communicative intent*. That is, for a communication device to be helpful, the user has to have some basic understanding of the communication process and must be intentional in expressing choices, desires, or needs.

For example, Maggie is a four-year-old who cannot speak. She communicates her wants and needs by using eyeblinks as responses to *yes* or *no* questions. When Maggie's dad asks her if she would like another glass of milk, she indicates her choice by raising her eyes up vertically for *yes* or moving her eyes down for *no*. Maggie clearly knows what she wants to communicate, she has a consistent method for making her wishes known, and she expects that her dad will understand her communication and act on it.

Dan communicates in a different way. He points to objects and makes gestures to show what he wants or needs. His gestures are clear and used consistently so that family members and even people who do not know Dan well can understand most of the time what he is communicating.

Shelley communicates very basic information about how she feels by crying when she is uncomfortable or wants attention and by laughing when she enjoys something like music, bright lights, or water running. Shelley does not, however, respond to *yes* or *no* questions. She does not make choices, even when objects are presented to her individually or in pairs. She cannot respond to a question like "Do you want some ice cream now?" Or "Would you like the teddy bear or the doll?"

Maggie and Dan may benefit from using some communication device because they are already using communication systems meaningfully and consistently. Shelley, however, may need to develop greater ability to communicate meaningfully before moving on to electronic communication.

Communication skills fall along a continuum. At one end of the continuum are very simple communications like expressing preferences by indicating *yes* or *no*, pointing or gesturing toward objects, or pointing to pictures. Use of sign is a more complex form of communication because it requires that the user understand that the signs are symbols for meaningful communications. Stringing together signs or words into meaningful phrases is an additional step toward more complex communication. When a person understands syntax and is aware of typical word order, this is another step forward. Each of these advances along the communication continuum represents a step toward more complex and sophisticated communication. Whatever assistive communication device is chosen should match or just slightly exceed the place on the continuum where the individual is functioning. It makes no sense, for example, to purchase an elaborate electronic communication device that requires understanding symbols and syntax when the individual using the device is just at the point of learning how to express *yes* and *no* preferences.

An electronic device does not teach communication; it enhances communication by giving audible or visible expression to thoughts that already exist or are being formed in the mind of the user.

Physical and Sensory Disabilities Are Not Barriers. Mastery of a few simple prerequisite skills is necessary before computers or electronic communication devices should be considered, but it is not necessary for a child to master *every* developmental milestone before entering the world of assistive technology. Physical or sensory disabilities can often be circumvented by the technology itself, and typical developmental milestones can sometimes be bypassed so that assistive technology can be used. For example, some educators assume that students cannot use computers until they have completely mastered keyboarding skills. This is a false assumption. Many students benefit from using computers, even though they operate the machine using a "hunt and peck" method or only one or two

---

Figure 2: Factors to Consider When Selecting Assistive Technology

Cognitive Factors	Motor Factors
Cognitive Abilities	Voluntary Motor Ability
Learning Disabilities	Involuntary Motor Ability
Attention Deficits	Fixed Posture & Positioning Needs
Sensory/Perceptual Difficulties	Recurring Purposeless Motion
Memory Problems	Motor Paralysis
Abstract Reasoning Ability	Low Muscle Tone
Problem-Solving Ability	Rigidity
	Spasticity
	Tremors

keys. In a similar fashion, students who have not mastered oral speech benefit from using augmentative communication devices while they continue to develop oral language.

Overall, the keys to knowing when to try assistive technology are (a) being realistic about the child's abilities and potential, (b) being open to trying the level of technology which meets the child where he or she is and (c) looking beyond the disability to see the child's possibilities.

Get a multidisciplinary evaluation.

Evaluations for assistive technology are not always easy to arrange. In many parts of the United States, there is no convenient center or "place" to go for an assessment. The available centers may be far away in another city or even another state. Since assistive technology is a new field, the systems for disseminating information and providing assistance are in the process of evolving. Parents may have to be "assistive technology detectives" in order to put together the information needed for a complete Assistive Technology evaluation for their child.

The place to start the evaluation is by considering the *functions* the child needs to perform and cannot because of the presence of a disability. The physicians, teachers, and therapists currently working with the child, as well as family members and friends who are around the child on a daily basis, can provide very valuable information about functional problems and potential solutions.

Finding Functional Solutions: The Solution Circle. The Alliance for Technology Access (ATA), a national network of assistive technology centers, has developed an informal method for using the functional information available from professionals, family members and friends as a basis for analyzing assistive technology needs. This process, called a Solution Circle, is a way to bring people together in an informal session that allows for creative thinking and is not inhibited by what is "legal," "currently available," or "what has been done before." The individual with a disability and 4-10 family members, professionals, and friends get together to brainstorm ideas about the technology which may help the individual perform functions that are hard, or impossible, to do because of disability. The Circle usually includes a balance between people who know the person who needs the technology and people who have specialized knowledge about technology, education, or work-related issues.

Solution Circle for Tom. To demonstrate how the Solution Circle works, let's take a look at how this process was used in the case of Tom, a high-school student with a learning disability. For Tom, the print in textbooks is a significant barrier to learning. Tom is "print disabled"; that is, he cannot read the printed word with much comprehension. Reading is a slow, unproductive process for him, even though he is intelligent and eager to learn. Tom and his parents were hoping that there might be a way that new technology could help Tom overcome or work around his problem with reading so that he could get more out of school and perhaps go on to college.

Tom's Solution Circle included his parents, Betty and Bob; his resource teacher; a friend Darrell; his soccer coach; his 4-H leader; and the owner of a local computer store. This group met together to think about how Tom could participate more fully in school and prepare himself for college, even though he could not read with comprehension past the second or third grade level.

Solution Circles generally take 1 to 1½ hours to complete. The steps include the following:

1. Star Time. The individual for whom the Solution Circle is being held is described in a holistic way. The emphasis is on how the individual is functioning at home and in the community. What does he or she like and dislike? What are his/her goals? Interests? If possible, the individual with a disability speaks for himself or herself or a video or pictures may be presented. The point of this part of the discussion is to give a clear picture of the individual as a whole person.

At Tom's Solution Circle, he explained his dream of going to college and becoming an agricultural botanist. Tom loves plants; he is interested in breeding new strains of wheat and perfecting various types of grain crops. Tom's 4-H leader agreed that Tom had real gifts in understanding plant growth and physiology, and that he already had sophisticated knowledge about botany which would prepare him well for college study.

2. Strengths. With a complete picture of the individual in mind, the group then makes an exhaustive list of the individual's strengths, particularly noting any technological accommodations which the individual is already using. What does the individual do well? What are his or her unimpaired functions? Often this discussion reveals an incredible number of adaptations that the individual has already achieved.

Tom's Solution Circle discovered that he had many strengths, including keen intelligence, perseverance, and thoroughness when approaching a task. Tom already had some effective learning strategies for remembering material that he heard. He had also learned to use a small tape recorder for keeping track of information provided in class.

3. Obstacles. With the individual's strengths in mind, the group then turns its attention to a consideration of the environment in which the individual is functioning and the activities in which the individual wants to participate but cannot at this time. The group considers what the obstacles and barriers might be for the individual in his or her environment and makes a list of these impediments.

For Tom, reading was a serious obstacle. He could not keep up with homework assignments because it took him so long to read his textbooks. In addition, he had difficulty reading directions on tests and often misread assignments on the blackboard.

4. The Enemy Within. Physical and cognitive impairments may pose difficult obstacles for an individual, but often the feelings that people have about the individual's disability or about assistive technology pose greater problems than the disabilities themselves. The Solution Circle process recognizes that human fears, concerns, reservations, and prejudices might stand in the way of a person's success as much as other types of limitations. Getting these fears and concerns out on the table often helps the group to deal more constructively with what is possible and what needs to be done.

One of the serious issues in Tom's situation was that his resource teacher felt he should continue to try to read for himself instead of relying on assistive technology. The teacher thought that if Tom did not have to read all the material, he would lose what little reading skill he had. In some ways, the teacher's opposition to considering assistive technology actually posed a greater barrier than the reading problem itself.

5. Solutions. The exciting part of a Solution Circle occurs when the group takes each obstacle or concern and turns it into a possible solution through the use of technology or some other type of adaptation. Not all solutions suggested eventually prove to be feasible, but the point of the discussion is to produce many possible solutions so that the individual and his or her family have an array of options from which to choose. With several people puzzling over the problems in a spirit of cooperation and collaboration, seemingly impossible barriers can be removed or conquered. The process recognizes the expertise and contributions of all participants, including the individual with disabilities and his or her family members. The freewheeling format of the discussion promotes ingenuity and innovation. All involved come away from a Solution Circle energized by the new possibilities.

Tom's Solution Circle became excited about the possibility of solving his reading problem by using computerized texts. The computer store operator mentioned he had heard that Recordings for the Blind offered textbooks on disk. Tom's parents got in touch with Recordings for the Blind and ordered texts for Tom to try on his computer at school. Soon Tom found that he could keep up with his classmates and study exactly the same material that they were covering. Because Tom had good strategies for memorizing information that he heard, he learned quickly from the texts that were read aloud to him by the computer. When given oral tests by his classroom teachers, he was able to recite appropriate answers which would have eluded him if he had had to read the tests for himself.

Technology has made all the difference for Tom; he has every reason to think that he will be able to go to college and pursue his intellectual interests. His resource teacher is now completely sold on the idea of assistive technology and using computerized books and wants to use the technique with other students. More than that, Tom's teacher also appreciates the process of the Solution Circle which allowed professionals and nonprofessionals to work together to find practical solutions without being too concerned about the formalities of the special education process. The informal nature of the Solution Circle validated the expertise of all the participants and gave everyone a chance to offer suggestions. The combination of a new process for planning and new technology made Tom a winner. This same combination holds potential for many students like Tom who benefit from technologies which eliminate barriers and open up new possibilities for learning.

From Function to Technology Solution. It happened that a participant in Tom's Solution Circle hit on a great idea for a solution to his functional problem with reading. At the suggestions of his Solution Circle, Tom began to use computerized books which he "reads" by having the computer speak the words as he follows along with the text. For Tom, computerized books proved to be a successful solution to his reading problem because they help him to get the information he needs without struggling with the reading process.

Not every Solution Circle will be like Tom's and identify the exact technology that the individual needs. But if a Solution Circle has worked well, the end result will be a clear analysis of the *functions* that need to be performed. This functional information can then be brought to technicians who can make suggestions for possible assistive technology solutions. There are over 50 assistive technology centers in the United States where knowledgeable individuals can assist people with disabilities and their families with making a match between functions that need to be performed and the technology that is available to perform those tasks. A list of assistive technology centers is available in the Appendix to this Guide.

Formal Assessment. Solution Circles are an effective, informal way to identify functional needs that can be met through technology. However, in the school setting, it is also necessary to establish a student's needs for technology in a more formal way. Formal evaluations for assistive technology must be multi-disciplinary, involving educators and therapists who are knowledgeable about the school curriculum and the particular types of needs that the student being assessed may have. For example, for a student with cerebral palsy the assistive technology evaluation might involve a teacher, a physical therapist, a speech and language clinician, and an occupational therapist. The teacher would assist the therapists in deter-

Figure 3: Assistive Technology Evaluation

INDIVIDUAL FUNCTIONAL ANALYSIS

Name _____ *Date* _____

COGNITIVE FACTORS
Cognitive Ability
Level of ability
Age appropriateness
Understanding of cause & effect
Paying Attention
Following prompts or directions
Handling of multi-step procedures
Filtering information
Staying on task
Perception
Needs lengthened response time
Requires multi-sensory input
Difficulty with rapid change
Significant visual/perceptual problems
Degree of visual-motor dexterity
Memory
Difficulty with recall
Requires reteaching learned skills
Requires repeated practice
Abstract Reasoning
Ability to analyze simple procedures
Ability to reproduce a sequence
Ability to analyze or synthesize information
Problem Solving
Ability to use prompts or cues to accomplish tasks
Ability to modify attempts and try another way

MOTOR FACTORS
Mobility
Needs help to be mobile
Needs motorized help to be independent
Needs help boarding transportation
Needs help to transfer independently
Cannot climb stairs
Needs help to open doors independently
Cannot carry materials in hands or arms
Cannot lift weight
Voluntary Motor
Limited control of head, trunk, or extremities
Visual motor problems
Fixed position and posture
Needs support to sit or stand
Needs adaptations in order to use technology
Motor Paralysis
Changes in muscle tone interfere in motor movements
Spastic movements result in poor control
Limited movement of head, arms or legs
Difficulty balancing in sitting position
Difficulty maintaining good posture
Low Muscle Tone
Limited use of arms or legs
Poor posture control
Fatigues quickly
Rigidity
Inhibits arm and leg movement

Inhibits balance to sit

Inhibits good posture

Spasticity

Limited upper range of motion

Limited lower range of motion

Interferes with accuracy and consistency of motor movements on one side

Tremors

Present all the time

Present when doing purposeful upper extremity task

Ability to compensate for tremors

Extraneous Movement

Athetoid (constant)

Ataxia (poor coordination in movement)

FINE MOTOR

Dexterity

Limited fine motor control

Has limited hand movement

Handwriting

Writing or copying ability

Degree of legibility

Interference with the pace of written work

Is frustrated by writing

Fatigue is a factor

Typing appears to be potentially faster than handwriting

SELF CARE

Needs assistance with going to the bathroom

Needs assistance to eat

Cannot take in food orally

Needs suctioning routinely

Has degenerative medical condition

Is medically fragile

Seizures limit alertness

Needs to rest frequently

Needs assistance to zip coat or tie shoes

COMMUNICATION

Receptive Language

Receptive language is significantly lower than ability

Receptive language is significantly higher than expressive

Expressive Language

Speech cannot be understood by others

Expressive language is significantly lower than ability

Mean Length of Utterance (MLU) is 3 words or less

Spontaneous or self initiated language is significantly limited

Does not make choices consistently

Does not respond appropriately with yes or no

SENSORY

Vision

Requires corrective lenses

Requires large print to read

Requires mobility training

Has blind spot

Cannot see at all

Hearing

Requires preferential seating

Hearing limitations affect the language thresholds

Requires assistance to receive language

Requires sign language to receive language

Has fluctuating hearing loss

Needs visual signals for safety purposes

mining what skills the student needed to learn and how technology might assist the student in acquiring those skills. Some assistive technology evaluations might require the additional services of an Audio Visual technician, adaptive physical education teacher, a rehabilitation counselor, or speech and language pathologist with specialized training in augmentative communication.

In school districts where there is no specialized expertise in technology and its applications, it may be necessary to contract for evaluations with special education cooperatives, medical centers, or centers that focus on technology assessment.

Individuals conducting an assistive technology evaluation should:

- Be knowledgeable about the student's strengths and weaknesses: medical needs, mobility, fine and gross motor skills, cognitive ability, communication abilities, vocational potential, self help needs, sensory abilities, level of academic achievement, and area(s) of disability;

- Have knowledge of and access to an array of assistive technology devices;

- Be familiar with the student's educational setting and educational needs;

- Be able to communicate effectively with parents and educators.

Because the assistive technology field is so new, there are no particular licenses or credentialing processes to identify a professional as qualified to do assistive technology evaluations. Generally speaking, individuals with professional licenses as occupational or physical therapists, special educators, speech pathologists, or rehabilitative counselors may have the expertise to conduct an Assistive Technology evaluation. When considering an evaluator, it is wise to ask about the evaluator's specific experience with assistive technology. It is also important to recognize that no one person or discipline will know everything about assistive technology; therefore, access to knowledgeable people at the local level and through other agencies, programs or services is essential.

Conducting the Assistive Technology Evaluation. The assistive technology evaluation must be tailored to the unique needs of the student. In some cases, the evaluation may be conducted by a team of individuals; in other cases, the evaluation may be conducted by a single individual (e.g., the speech pathologist). Questions to be addressed during the assessment should be related to the specific tasks the student needs to be able to perform and what, if any, assistive technology would help. The following questions may be considered during the assessment:

- What tasks does the student need to perform that he or she cannot perform?

- Is there a low tech device which will address the student's needs satisfactorily?

- What types of high tech assistive devices may help the student in performing the task?

- Will assistive technology help the student to perform the task in the least restrictive environment?

- Is the device being considered suited to the student's educational needs and abilities?

- Will the assistive technology device remain suitable over time?

- How long lasting will this solution potentially be?

These are only a few of the considerations which need to be addressed as part of the evaluation process. There is no specific "test" for evaluating the need for assistive technology. Therefore, prior to conducting the evaluation, the individuals doing the assessment need to have a well planned process in mind.

The formal written assistive technology evaluation report should address, but not be limited to, the following points:

- Procedures used to evaluate the student's needs;

- Instruments employed in the evaluation, assuring that a range of levels of technologies has been considered;

- Results of evaluations, including both qualitative and quantitative measures;

- Recommendations for levels of technology appropriate to the student's capabilities and potentials, and

- Implications for educational programming, including discussion of both individual technology needs and recommended environmental and instructional modifications.

In the end, an assistive technology evaluation should provide recommendations for accommodations, adaptations, devices, and services based on the individual's strengths, needs, and preferred lifestyle. The evaluation should indicate (a) whether devices and services have potential for improving function, and (b) what training may be necessary in order to use the technology equipment safely and effectively.

Examine available technology with a critical eye. It is easy to be dazzled by the possibilities in new assistive technology, but it is important for parents to be wise consumers and ask probing questions about the features and quality of an assistive technology device.

The following is a list of questions to consider when evaluating a particular assistive technology device:

Performance

Does it work efficiently and effectively?

Is it easy to learn to use this device?

Is it compatible with other devices?

Does this device serve only one purpose or is it flexible?

"Elegance"

Does this device represent the simplest, most efficient way to accomplish the task?

Or is this device too elaborate, too complicated to be worthwhile?

Ergonomics

Does it fit the individual?

Is it convenient to use in the environment?

Is the equipment portable enough to go where the user goes?

Are different devices needed in different environments?

Reliability

What is the manufacturer's reputation for reliability?

Does it stand up well to normal use?

Is it durable?

Safety

Is it safe to use?

What is the power source for the device? Is it safe?

Is a margin built in for foreseeable misuse?

Practicality

Do company sales people seem knowledgeable and helpful?

Are the company's service people knowledgeable and helpful?

Does the device have a warranty? How long is the device guaranteed to function?

How available are repair services? At what cost?

Can this device be leased?

Is this device available for a trial period before purchase?

Will this device soon be outdated? Is something better on the horizon?

Will the company update the device?

Does the manufacturer provide training in using the device?

Aesthetics

Is this device attractive to the eye?

Does the device fit well into the user's lifestyle?

Normalization

Does the device assist the user with more normalized living? Can the user operate the device independently or with a minimum of assistance?

Or does the device "stick out" too much and advertise the disability of the user?

Does the equipment minimize difference or exaggerate difference?

Does the device have the potential to increase the quantity and quality of time spent with nondisabled peers? Or does the device separate the user from others?

Cost effectiveness

Do the benefits the device provides justify the cost?

Are there less expensive devices or models that serve the purpose as well?

Personal acceptance

Is this device the user's own choice?

Does the potential user like this device and want to use it?

Does the potential user view this device as life-enhancing?

Would the user have preferred some other device or means to perform the task?

Will using the device always be a chore or can using it become a habit?

There are several ways that consumers can find answers to their specific questions about assistive technology devices. Most vendors will provide good basic information about the product. Call the vendor and ask for brochures, product specifications, price list and any other written information. This is a place to start. A second step is to read reviews of the product in trade magazines or Closing the Gap, a widely respected publication that reviews new assistive technology products. If possible, it is very helpful to talk to other consumers who are already using the product. Ask them about the pros and cons of using the device. Then visit a preview center, if there is one nearby, and try out several types of devices. Ask for general recommendations from the preview center's staff. After identifying a device that appears to meet the potential user's needs, try the device out for a month to six weeks to make sure that it performs as advertised and fits in well with the user's lifestyle. During the trial period, it will be possible to identify training needs for the user, family members and school staff. The trial period will also be a time for the user to test the device in several settings to determine its portability and flexibility.

Match the Individual's Needs to Specific Equipment Features.

When considering an assistive technology device, it is very important to consider how a device matches up with the particular individual's needs and habits. In some ways, an assistive device becomes an extension of the user's mind and body. As such, it is a highly personal item. A device may work as advertised, but still not meet an individual's needs because the individual just does not feel "comfortable" in using it.

Example: Cindy, a fourteen-year-old who is blind and has mild cerebral palsy affecting her hands and arms, was being taught Morse Code as a means to speed up her writing. Cindy had difficulty using a Brailler because her arm strength was so limited, her teacher thought Morse Code would be an easier method of writing for Cindy. The only problem was that Cindy did not like using Morse Code. To her, it seemed as if she was having to learn another complicated language when she already knew Braille and liked to use it. Cindy admitted that writing in Braille was slow for her but she was more comfortable with it. Cindy and her teacher were at an impasse until a friend suggested to Cindy that she try writing on a voice-output computer. Cindy loved the computer! With a headset attached to the sound system, she could listen carefully to the computer as it read aloud the letters and words she was typing on a light touch, tactile-marked keyboard. This computer also had a feature of printing out text in either standard print or Braille. Cindy was delighted—she could write copy for herself to read in Braille and for her sighted teachers to read in regular print. This solution worked because it met Cindy's learning needs and responded to her own ideas about herself. She did not want to use Morse Code because it was a separate type of communication known only to a few. With her computer, voiced software, and dual printer, she had the best of two worlds—she could "hear" her writing as she typed, she could read it over in Braille, and her sighted teachers could read her finished product. This solution helped Cindy to improve her composition skills, speed up her writing time, and communicate more easily with sighted people.

Cindy was fortunate because her assistive technology solution met her needs almost perfectly. Such a close match is not, however,

Figure 4: Assistive Technology Evaluation

DEVICE OR EQUIPMENT FEATURES OR FUNCTIONS

Name _____ *Date* _____

Motor/Self Care
manual wheelchair
power wheelchair
bus lift
supportive classroom chair
stander
walker
lift for transfers
positioning device
canes or crutches
adapted commode
suctioning device
braces or supports
other: _____

Fine Motor
word processor
word processor with prediction
voiced word processor with prediction
adapted keyboard
keyguard
alternative key arrangement
voice activated computer access
infrared computer access
mouse access
trackball
joystick
power pad
switch (e.g., mouth, lip, chin)
touch screen
pointers
drag and click desk accessory
sticky keys
onscreen keyboard

printer for written work
adapted feeding utensils
braces or splints
other: _____

Cognitive/Communication
communication board(s)
communication wallet
total communication
manual sign
word processor with voice
programmed voice output
icon prediction
electronic communication device
programmable switch with voice output
no-reading-necessary word processor
spell checker
grammar checker
outlining program
other: _____

Sensory/Perceptual
hearing aid(s)
classroom amplification
boosted signal to noise ratio (e.g., headset to keep focus during word processing)
corrective lenses
enlarged print
taped books
voiced word processing
voiced screen directions
CCTV
other: _____

always possible. Nonetheless, every effort should be made to have the match be as close as it can be. In general, when assistive technology solutions are individualized, simple to use, and responsive to the whole person, they are more likely to be used by the individual. When the device performs a task well, but does not "fit" the individual, the technology is likely to be abandoned by the user in favor of something else which meets the need more exactly. Too often devices are purchased because of their technical potential without thought to their relationship to the individual and his or her lifestyle. These mismatched devices are the ones that end up languishing in their packing boxes—a sad reminder of time and money spent to no avail.

Try the Device Before Buying.

It cannot be emphasized enough how vital it is to try out assistive technology devices and equipment before buying. Trying out a device for several weeks provides the user with an opportunity to learn how to use the device and how to adapt to its features while at the same time testing the device in the various environments where it will be used.

Example 1: Mike tried out a communication device which attached nicely to his wheelchair tray and was compatible with the computer that he used for doing school work. Though the communication device worked well and was relatively easy to program, Mike found out quickly that the device was just too bulky to be useful for him. When he traveled around the school, the communication device blocked his view of the terrain and of people passing by. He found he missed opportunities to communicate because he could not see who was coming his way. Mike also discovered that the communication device did not serve him well in crowds like those at pep rallies or basketball games. After a month of working with this communication device, Mike decided it was not for him and selected instead a device that was less complicated, smaller, and more portable. The second device was not as sophisticated as the first, but it better met his needs for quick communication with friends in social settings. If he had not had the opportunity to try out both devices for an extended period of time, Mike might not have realized the value of the second device and may have been stuck with a communication device that was too large and too sophisticated to match his lifestyle.

Example 2: Similarly, Marilyn benefited from a trial period with her communication device. She found out the first week that the particular device she had chosen would not work for her because it broke too easily and it was difficult to get repaired. During the first week that Marilyn had the device for trial, her teacher broke one of the buttons during a programming session. It took two weeks to contact the manufacturer and then the device had to be mailed back to the factory for repairs. The device was gone for over six weeks, and the manufacturer would not supply a "loaner" while Marilyn waited for repairs to the first device. This experience taught Marilyn the importance of having a responsive manufacturer who is willing to repair devices quickly and to supply substitutes for the user while repairs are being made. Marilyn decided on a different device with similar features and a great helpline to provide assistance with the maintenance of the machine.

The information that can be learned during a trial period with a device is invaluable to the user. It is discouraging to find out during the trial that a device is not all it is purported to be or that it does not work as well as advertised. It is far better to learn before purchase that a device does not meet the user's needs than to learn after purchase and be stuck with an expensive, unusable machine. For the consumer, it is daunting to think about starting over again with the process of selecting a device. Nonetheless, it is worthwhile to seek more information and look again. Having been through a trial, even when the outcome is not successful, provides the user with greater clarity about what an appropriate device will have to be able to do. The second time around the search is likely to go faster and come out with a better result.

Identify Next Steps.

Once a device has been selected, the consumer becomes impatient to have one and begin using it right away. But at this point, important work still needs to be done. Funding the device is a major consideration. Sometimes families will pay for the device themselves, but under other circumstances, the device will be purchased by a school district, through Medicaid or private insurance, or through some other means. Parents need to become familiar with the various funding options and determine which one will work for them. (See "Funding Assistive Technology," p. 00, for additional information about funding sources).

Also when considering funding, families should think about costs beyond the price of the device itself. For example, a computer set-up with a keyboard, monitor and printer might cost $3,500. This equipment is basically useless unless other equipment is purchased as well: software, adaptive devices, paper, manuals, upgrades. Prices for these additions can raise the actual cost of the device by hundreds of dollars.

Devices often require training for the user, family members, and others to ensure effective and safe use. How much does training cost? Who will provide it? Repair and maintenance are other costs usually additional to the price of the equipment. Sometimes families will also want to insure the assistive device so insurance payments become part of the overall cost.

Since making an assistive technology purchase is such an important personal and financial decision, it is wise to have a realistic budget in mind that includes all of the equipment and services that are necessary to make the assistive technology work effectively. With this budget in mind, it becomes easier to plan the purchase, seek out funding sources, and make a compelling case for financial assistance.

Determine What Follow-up Is Needed.

After the assistive technology device has been purchased and put to use, there are additional follow-up activities that need to take place. The original assistive technology evaluation should include a way to monitor the use of the device. Periodic scheduled reviews by the evaluator, follow-up calls to and from the family are some ways to help assure effective, safe use. Families who travel great distances for evaluation need to be certain that services like maintenance, repair and replacement of devices are available within a reasonable distance from home.

Assistive technology devices are used best when all the people in the life of the individual with disabilities understand the devices in the same way. At first, devices may seem to exaggerate differences between a person and the rest of the world. Care should be taken to explain that assistive equipment is a difference equalizer, not a difference maker. Classmates and friends need to understand that the adapted seating or adapted keyboard helps the individual do what other students do. Adults in a child's life need to understand that devices work to make life easier, better, and more functional. People need to know that ramps help keep individuals with mobility disabilities from being separated from peers; that communication technology allows people to "speak" their thoughts.

Close communication between parents and their child's helpers—teachers, therapists, day care workers and others—is essential to make sure devices and services are being used safely and effectively. If the device is working well, but the child is not being integrated into the classroom or other environments, then there may be a need for additional training for the children and adults who interact with the child.

Besides keeping track of how the device is working and being used, it is important to observe progress in the areas of technology which are useful to the individual with the assistive technology device. As upgrades of equipment occur or more sophisticated models come on the market, the user may want to consider modifying or replacing the equipment that is currently in use. Also as the individual becomes more skilled at using technology, the individual may outgrow the current device and need to look for more advanced equipment. It can be assumed with most high tech items that in three to five years there will be a need for upgrade or replacement. The wise consumer begins early to plan for the next step in technology, including saving money for a new device and staying alert to the new options that become available.

What kinds of training need to occur when a child has a new assistive technology device?

Because assistive technology of the high tech variety is so new, it is particularly important that training be provided to all those who may need it. In the school setting, it is helpful for all educators and administrators to have some awareness training so that they have a general idea of what assistive technology is. Areas to be covered in inservice training might include:

- Legal issues related to assistive technology

- Awareness training concerning how to serve students with assistive technology needs

- Information on how assistive technology relates to the evaluation process

- How to write IEPs for students who require use of assistive technology devices
- The relationship between technology and student placement
- The nature of common assistive technology devices
- Resources to contact for information on assistive technology.

Beyond these awareness activities, those members of the school staff who work directly with a student who uses technology need to have training on the specifics of using the device and how it is maintained and serviced. Training should include, but not be limited to, the following:

- Review of the student's educational and assistive technology needs.
- Review of goals and objectives, supplementary aids and services, and related services on the IEP or IFSP.
- Training on how to use and maintain the device.
- Training on proper transport of the device within the school building and from home to school.
- Training on how to program the device, if needed.
- Training on how to use the device effectively during instruction.
- Training in troubleshooting when the device is not working properly.
- Information about what to do when the device is not functioning or broken.
- Information about how to coordinate assistive technology with all the activities in the student's day.
- Training in methods to evaluate the effectiveness of assistive technology.

Depending on the student's needs and the type of assistive technology used by the student, it may be advantageous for assistive technology information to be shared with the student's peers. Such training will help fellow students to gain an understanding of the student's assistive device, foster acceptance in the social environment, and reduce fears other students may have about socializing with the student who uses technology. In some cases, parents and the student may want to be involved in the peer training.

Parents may require training, too, in order for the device to be used at home for the student to complete homework assignments or participate in extended school year services. Once trained, the parents can become a resource to the student for proper care and maintenance of the device.

Most importantly, the student himself or herself, will need training in how to use the device as independently as possible. Training for the student may be written into the IEP as a separate goal or may be included as a related service that supports the student's special education program.

SUMMARY

Purchasing a high tech assistive technology device is a major life decision because of the potential impact on the individual and because such devices can be costly. When considering an assistive technology device, it is important to do the following:

- Be realistic about the user's capabilities and needs; get a multi-disciplinary evaluation;

- Examine available technology with a critical eye;

- Match the individual's needs to specific equipment features;

- Test the device for a trial period;

- Identify next steps;
- Determine what needs to be done for follow-up after purchase.

Evaluations for assistive technology, both informal and formal, should consider first of all the functions that the user wishes to perform using technology.

When evaluating a particular piece of equipment, consideration should be given to the following features:

- performance
- simplicity of design
- ergonomics
- reliability
- safety
- practicality
- aesthetics
- normalization
- cost effectiveness
- personal acceptance

Good sources of information about assistive devices are manufacturers' publications, trade journals, preview centers, and consumers who are already using the device.

Once a device is selected, the consumer will need to secure funding for the purchase and be aware of additional costs for related equipment, insurance and training.

KEY POINTS

The student's needs must be balanced with other factors to choose technology that is best for the student. These factors include:

- student's needs;
- student's likes;
- student's gender and age;
- student's home and family activities;
- student getting to and from school (or wherever services are provided);
- student's job hopes;
- range of technologies available;
- features of the technology;
- cost of the technology;
- how the technology is to be used;
- dependability of the technology;
- ease with which the technology can be moved;
- length of time the technology will last;
- usefulness of the technology with other devices;
- ability of the student to try out the technology;
- ease with which the technology can be maintained;
- safety of student from injury;
- protection from theft and damage;
- student's feelings about the technology;
- comfort of the technology;

- ease with which the technology can be repaired, and parents' ability to repair the technology; and

- ease with which the technology can be put together.

HINTS FOR PARENTS

Don't let the cost of assistive technology deter you from considering it for your child. High tech assistive technology can be quite costly, but it can also make the difference for your child in terms of becoming well educated, employable, and a fully included member of the community. Don't leave any stone unturned when looking for funding sources. Consider any or all of the following for funding or assistance:

- Early intervention programs

- Schools

- Transition programs

- Vocational Rehabilitation

- State Programs for Children with Special Health Care Needs

- Medicaid

- Medicare

- State Technology Resources

- Used Equipment

- Leasing

- Equipment Loan Programs

- Disability Organizations

A CHILD'S SITUATION TO CONSIDER: SIERRA

Sierra wants to play with dolls like other children her age, but she has a muscle disease that has caused her to lose muscle tone except in one hand.

- What could be done to allow Sierra to dress and undress her dolls, comb their hair, and bathe them?

Sierra's Solution

The assistive technology solution for Sierra involved her whole family. While vacationing in Mexico, Sierra's grandmother found her a fashion doll that was a bit larger than the typical "Barbie doll." The larger doll was easier for Sierra to manipulate. Sierra's mother sewed several outfits for the doll using velcro instead of snaps or buttons as fasteners.

Sierra's dad bought doll stands at a toy store and fastened several stands with clamps to Sierra's wheelchair tray. He also fastened a plastic pouch to the tray. Sierra puts the small doll accessories in the pouch. When Sierra wants to dress her doll, she puts the doll in one of the stands. In this way, the doll is held securely and Sierra can dress and undress the doll with one hand.

Sierra's friends also use the doll stands for their dolls. With this arrangement, two or three girls can play together.

Solution Summary
Larger doll
Velcro fasteners
Plastic pouch
Doll stands
Clamps

CHAPTER 3

Funding Assistive Technology

Funding for assistive technology is available from a variety of public and private sources. To receive public or private funding, the individual must meet eligibility criteria for the specific program and provide sufficient documentation of the need for assistive technology.

The following list includes some of the programs which may pay for equipment if the individual needing the device meets their requirements. Many of these programs are run by different agencies in different states, making them hard to find. In general, the state's Tech Act office can assist consumers and family members in finding and using these programs (See Appendix under Resources).

PUBLIC PROGRAMS

Early Intervention Programs (Individuals with Disabilities Education Act)

Young children (0-3) and their families may receive help through early intervention programs in evaluating what the child needs, in getting assistive technology, and in learning how to use it. Equipment and services must be included in a written plan, called an Individualized Family Service Plan (IFSP). To find the program for a particular state, call National Early Childhood Technical Assistance System (NEC*TAS) at 919-962-2001 or 919-966-4041 (TDD) for those with speech or hearing problems.

Head Start

This child development program provides comprehensive educational and health services for eligible children ages 3-5. Since 1982, federal law has required that at least 10 percent of the total number of placements must be available to children who are disabled and require special services. Head Start is a mainstream placement option for children whose IEP calls for placement with nondisabled children. The January 1993 Head Start regulations specifically require the consideration of assistive technology services and devices. For more information, contact National Head Start Association, 201 N. Union St., Suite 320, Alexandria, VA 22314; 703-739-0875.

Schools (IDEA, Part B)

This program mandates a free, appropriate public education for preschoolers, children and youth with disabilities. An Individualized Education Program (IEP) is required for all children with a disability. These children are entitled to special education, related services or supplementary aids. If the IEP team determines that assistive technology is required for a free, appropriate public education, then it must be provided at no cost to the child. The technology must be included in the child's Individualized Education Program (IEP). Parents have a right to be involved and should help to develop the IEP goals which may include technology. For help in getting assistive technology in the IEP, call the Parents, Let's Unite for Kids (PLUK) office at 1-800-222-7585.

State Operated and Supported Schools (Chapter I)

This program provides federal assistance to help educate children with disabilities who are enrolled in state-operated and state-supported programs. Federal funds must be used to pay for services that supplement a child's basic special education program, such as construction and the purchase of equipment. For more information, contact your State Department of Education.

Section 504 of the Rehabilitation Act of 1 1973

Section 504 is a civil-rights mandate that requires accommodations for students who have disabilities that nevertheless do not qualify them for special education services. It denies federal funds to any institution, including a school, whose practices or policies discriminate against individuals with disabilities. This legislation has resulted in a number of outcomes, including various actions to remove physical barriers to education, which may incorporate assistive technology. For more information, contact the nearest regional Office of Civil Rights or the State Vocational Rehabilitation Agency.

State Programs for Children with Special Health Care Needs (CSHCN)

These programs provide and pay for services for eligible children. CSHCN programs vary widely from state to state in the services they offer, the number of children served, and the requirements for eligibility. Some CSHCN programs do pay for assistive technology devices when no other funding source is available and the equipment is necessary for health-related reasons. Most CSHCN programs are run by the state health agency. To contact CSHCN, ask Information for the telephone number of the state health agency.

School-to-Work Transition Programs

Transition programs are charged with assisting students with disabilities to receive job related training and placement services to help them move from school to work. Sometimes assistive technology may be necessary in order for a student to make a successful transition and become employable. If technology is needed for transition purposes, it can be written into the student's Individualized Transition Plan (ITP). To receive more information about transition and technology, call the Parent Training and Information Center (PTI) in your state (See Appendix).

Vocational Rehabilitation Services

State vocational rehabilitation agencies provide information, evaluation services, training and funding for technology and education to help adults go to work or live more independently. If technology is necessary for an individual to work, Vocational Rehabilitation may pay for the equipment as part of an Individualized Work-Related Plan (IWRP). To locate the nearest Vocational Rehabilitation Agency, look in the telephone book under state government.

Plan to Achieve Self-Support (PASS)

One of many Social Security Administration work incentive programs, this program provides an income and resource exclusion that allows a blind or disabled person to set aside income and resources for a work goal such as education, equipment purchase, vocational training and starting a business. It should be considered for all students with vocational goals who are receiving social security benefits.

This program provides a mechanism for people to set aside funds to purchase work-related equipment, such as assistive technology devices and services. In many cases, if an individual is a recipient of SSI and writes a PASS to purchase education or equipment, an additional SSI check will be provided to cover other living expenses. Sometimes if a person receives Social Security Disability Insurance (SSDI) and designs a PASS, it may make the individual eligible for SSI because the SSDI has been allocated for equipment and services.

Impairment-Related Work Expense (IRWE)

Impairment-Related Work Expense (IRWE)—one of the Social Security Administration's work incentive programs—allows an employed individual with a disability who receives or is eligible for SSI or SSDI to deduct work-related expenses from reported gross income.

This deduction allows the person to continue drawing SSDI or SSI and associated benefits (Medicaid or Medicare) if the IRWE deduction reduces earning below the Substantial Gainful Activity (SGA) Test.

Although this method does not provide funding to pay for a device or service, it is a way of allowing the use of the individual's own money to pay for assistive devices and services necessary to return to work. The following is a list of possible work-related expenses: special transportation to and from work, personal assistance on the job, structural modifications, durable medical equipment, prostheses, medical supplies and services, work-related equipment, non-medical appliances and equipment, routine drug and medical costs, and diagnostic procedure costs.

Medicaid

Medicaid is a joint federal and state program which covers some equipment if it is considered medically necessary. For more information about Medicaid and who and what is covered, contact the local Department of Human Services office.

Medicare

Although not a usual source of funds for assistive technology, Part B of Medicare provides coverage for some durable medical equipment if it is considered medically necessary and is for use in the person's home. For more information about Medicare benefits, contact the Social Security Administration Regional Office.

Technology-Related Assistance for Individuals with Disabilities Act of 1988

This federal competitive grants program provides monies for states to establish a statewide, consumer-responsive service delivery system designed to effect systems change regarding assistive technology. In most Tech Act states, a funding specialist or policy analyst is available to assist with accessing assistive technology. Several states operate loan programs to help with the purchase of devices and services. For more information, contact RESNA Technology Assistance Project, 1700 N. Moore St., Suite 1540, Arlington VA 22209-1903; 703-524-6686.

PRIVATE PROGRAMS

Private Insurance

Some health insurance plans will buy equipment, but it depends on the specific wording of the policy. Unless the policy says the equipment is not covered, it makes sense to ask the insurance company to pay for it. The equipment must be considered *medically necessary* and therefore requires a doctor's prescription.

Loans

There are several low or no interest loans available to help buy technology. Call the state Tech Act program or the manufacturer of the equipment may know where to get this type of loan.

Non-Profit Disability Associations

There are many disability organizations, some of which may be able to loan equipment or provide information about other funding sources or support groups. These organizations include: National Easter Seal Society, March of Dimes, Muscular Dystrophy Association, United Way, United Cerebral Palsy Association, and the Braille Institute.

Foundations

Some private foundations have been set up specifically to provide help to people with disabilities. A listing of such foundations can be found at the library or may be available from the state Tech Act program.

Programs Providing Assistive Technology

The state Tech Act programs offer referrals for evaluation and equipment recommendations as well as assistance with identifying funding or equipment lending sources. A therapy department in a local hospital or Disabled Students Center at a local college or university may also offer to help locate technology programs in the area. Alliance for Technology Access Centers (ATA) sometimes have loan programs or information about purchasing used equipment or renting equipment.

Civic Organizations

There are many local civic and service organizations which may provide money to help someone in their community. Lists of these organizations are available from the Chamber of Commerce. Examples of these organizations are: Lions Club, Masons, Grotto, Veterans of Foreign Wars (VFW), Elks Club, Rotary Club, Kiwanis, Knights of Columbus and Soroptomists. Some of these organizations have a national focus on disability or on a particular disability. Others will fund devices for a particular child who is known to the local club.

Charities and Fund-Raisers

Local churches, high school groups, neighborhood organizations, labor unions, or special interest groups (e.g., computer clubs, ham operators) may plan a fund-raiser to help purchase assistive technology. College student organizations (fraternities and sororities) may give money or students' time to help a special cause. Even if money is not available, they may be willing to help organize a fund raiser.

Local media (radio, television, newspapers) sometimes will sponsor fund-raising activities to fund devices. They may not contribute money but will help with organizing the fund-raising activity and publicizing it to the community.

OTHER OPTIONS

In addition to federal and private funding sources, there are education-related grants, corporate technology donation programs, and funding options that consumers should consider. Information on these alternative options is available through a number of sources, including the following:

Newsletters

- *Education Grants Alert*, Capital Publications Inc., P.O. Box 1453, Alexandria VA 22313-2052; 800-655-5597.

- *Education Technology News*, Business Publishers Inc, 951 Pershing Dr., Silver Spring MD 20910-4464; 301-5878-6300.

- *Financing Assistive Technology*, Smiling Interface, P.O. Box 2792, Church St. Station, New York NY 10008-2792; 415-864-2220.

- *Special Education Report*, Capital Publications Inc., P.O. Box 1453, Alexandria VA 22313-2053; 800-655-5597.

- *Technology and Learning*, Peter Li Inc. Publishing, 330 Progress Rd., Dayton OH 45449; 415-457-4333.

Technology Manufacturers

If it is not possible financially to purchase equipment, consumers can sometimes rent or borrow equipment directly from the manufacturer.

Used Equipment

Used equipment is often advertised for sale in disability-related publications, or the consumer can place a newspaper ad to see if used equipment can be purchased locally. Several companies refurbish old computers and sell them at low prices. Listings of used computer outlets can be obtained from ATA Centers or state Tech Act programs.

Leasing

Many manufacturers of assistive technology devices have equipment which is available for rent or lease. Sometimes the rent or lease payments can be applied toward purchase. Check with the manufacturer to see if this is an option.

Equipment Loan Programs

Many states have equipment loan programs as do some rehabilitation facilities and disability organizations. Information about loan programs is available from Tech Act programs.

HOW TO APPLY FOR FUNDING

There is an art to applying for funding for assistive technology. It is necessary to use just the right words to suit the particular agency that might be the funding source. It is also crucial to document the need for and projected outcome of assistive technology. This documentation should include at minimum:

- A written statement of medical need from doctors or other health professionals. If the child had an evaluation by a rehabilitation professional, also include this report.

- A description of the child's needs resulting from the disability. This description can come from the doctor or other professional who evaluated the child.

- Description of how the technology helps the child. For example, the equipment may improve the safety for the child or allow the child to do things more independently. Be sure to point out how money will be saved if use of the equipment allows attendant care to be reduced.

- A clear statement based on assessment information that the child is a good candidate who has the cognitive and physical capacities necessary for using the technology.

In summary, the documentation to support an assistive technology funding request should include a physician's prescription, the child's assessment, an explanation of projected benefit from use of the technology or service, and any correspondence obtained from professionals that would support the child's need for technology.

The initial funding request should include not only the cost of the device, but also the cost of ongoing support and instruction in the use of the technology. Assistive devices often have "hidden" expenses that are incurred with their purchase, and these expenses are frequently costly over time. Battery-powered devices may require frequent charging or cleaning. Upgrades for computer software may be necessary. Special modifications of the home or school environment may be necessary for the technology to be used. In each of these examples, costs associated with the technology may have to be assumed by the family if they are not considered in the initial application for funding.

It is also helpful to include with the funding request a picture or a descriptive brochure about the device being requested. This is important because often persons who are reviewing the application do not know about the wide range of technologies that might be appropriate.

Appropriate wording on the application is absolutely necessary. Key concepts for Medicaid include "medical necessity" and "restore the patient to his or her best functional level." The term *medical necessity* means that the device is included in the course of treatment being provided to the child and that a professional, such as a physician or speech therapist, is supervising its use. Medicaid and private insurers alike generally pay for technologies that help restore people to "functioning levels" and take the place of a body part that is not working. Typically, these programs do not pay for technologies or services whose function is educational or life-enhancing rather than health-related.

The key for private insurance is "terms of the policy." It must be remembered that coverage by any insurance company does not set a precedent. Just because one child receives needed technology under a particular policy issued by a company does not mean that all other covered children will also have technology paid for by that company. Each application stands on its own based on the expressed terms of the policy.

It is usually under the major medical provisions of a health policy that assistive technology can be provided as "other medical services and supplies." It may, however, be necessary to purchase additional insurance coverage or a "rider" in order for technology costs to be included in the terms of the policy. It is important to remember that health insurance policies are oriented toward health care, and not toward changes in the environment or rehabilitation.

Both private health insurance policies and Medicaid sometimes impose limits on the number of assistive technology devices over a certain cost that can be purchased within a certain time frame. Sometimes the rule is that the funding source will purchase only one device in the individual's lifetime. With these kinds of restrictions, it is all the more critical to be sure that the technology choice is the right one.

Tips That Lead To Success

- Apply to several funding sources at the same time. Be sure to meet the requirements of each agency.

- Find out if agencies will share costs.

- Fill in the agency's forms correctly. Many applications are denied because forms are not filled out properly.

- In addition to the standard form, include any other information that describes or shows what the equipment does and how it benefits the child. Assume no knowledge on the part of the reviewers.

- Turn in all documentation at the same time.

- Avoid using jargon; define all unfamiliar terms.

- Take the funding request package to the agency in person. While there, have it checked to make sure everything required has been included. Get the name of the person who reviewed the application.

- Call regularly to check on the funding request; each time try to talk to the same person.

- Be super polite—and persistent!

WHAT IF FUNDING IS DENIED?

It is not at all unusual for an initial funding request to be denied. Even when family members and professionals have been meticulous in preparing applications requesting funding for needed technology, denials should be anticipated. Making an appeal is worth the effort since many denials are reversed at the appeal level.

To start the appeal process, obtain any documentation or information provided by the funding agency (e.g., Medicaid or the private insurance company) relating to appeal procedures: forms to use, timelines, and filing procedures, for instance. This information will help in the prompt preparation for appeal. The kind of appeal to be made depends on the reason for denial. When developing an appeal, find out the following:

- Why the request was denied. Ask for the reason in writing. Sometimes requests are denied because a reviewer lacks understanding of the technology or there may be an error in the paperwork.

- If needed, correct any mistakes or include more information; then resubmit the request.

Going to appeal makes sense because generally the appeal places the application before more experienced persons in the decision-making hierarchy. The technology requested is often new, and the initial examiners in the process may be unaware of its usefulness. Also, insufficient documentation may have been provided in the original application, and the problem can be remedied on appeal.

Don't be daunted by the length of the appeal process. Follow it through to its completion. In some states, families may be able to appeal a denial beyond the first level. For example, some states have "unfair claims settlement practices" regulations, which are administered through the insurance commissioner's office.

Always make your appeal in person and take the child and the equipment if possible. If only part of the money is offered by one agency, ask another agency to share costs. If the appeal is denied, try again. Submit the funding request to another agency. Being persistent will nearly always result in success.

When going through the appeal process, turn to the state Protection and Advocacy Program (P & A) for guidance and support. P & A advocates can help make sure that a child's rights to technology and related services are not denied.

Who pays when assistive technology is needed at school?

The party who is responsible for paying for assistive technology depends upon the circumstances under which the technology is purchased. Under the special education law, students with disabilities who are eligible for special education are entitled to a free appropriate public education. Parents do not have to pay for school services, including assistive technology, if that service is part of the student's Individualized Education Program (IEP). If the student is eligible for Medicaid, the school district can request that Medicaid pay for the device. If parents choose to do so, they may agree to use private insurance to pay for a device that is used at school. Parents cannot, however, be forced to use their insurance in this way. If the private insurance requires a co-payment, the school district would have to pay this amount since parents should not have to pay any special education related costs.

Does Section 504 pay for assistive technology?

Section 504, part of the Rehabilitation Act of 1973, is civil rights legislation intended to prevent discrimination against individuals with disabilities in any program which receives federal funding. Students with disabilities, who nevertheless do not qualify for special education, may still be eligible for accommodations under Section 504 of the Rehabilitation Act of 1973. Section 504, however, does not provide any funding for accommodations.

Like the special education law, Section 504 requires public schools to provide students with disabilities with a free appropriate public education and, in addition, ensures that students with disabilities are afforded an equal opportunity to participate in school programs. This means that schools may need to make special arrangements so that students with disabilities have access to the full range of programs and activities offered. For example, a student who needs a wheelchair lift on a school bus must be provided with this technology. Other modifications which might be required under Section 504 include installing ramps into buildings and modifying bathrooms to provide access for individuals with physical disabilities. Even though required by the law, none of these types of modifications would be funded by Section 504.

Under what circumstances does private health insurance pay for assistive technology?

Some private health insurance policies will pay all or part of the cost for some assistive technology devices. The devices are unlikely to be listed specifically in the policy, but may be included under some generic term like "therapeutic aids." Usually the devices have to be prescribed by a physician to be covered.

When does Medicaid cover assistive technology?

Medicaid (Title XIX) will pay for "prosthetic devices," that is, replacement, corrective, or supportive devices prescribed by a physician or other licensed person. Each state has some flexibility in determining which prosthetic devices it will include in its list of Medicaid covered expenses. Devices that are frequently covered by Medicaid are canes, crutches, walkers, manual wheelchairs, hospital beds, and hearing aids or eyeglasses for children and youth. Some state Medicaid programs cover augmentative communication devices.

SUMMARY

Assistive technology can be expensive to purchase, but there are public and private sources for funding devices. Common public funding sources include: early childhood intervention programs, schools, Vocational Rehabilitation, and Medicaid. Private sources may involve health insurance, personal loans, charitable donations, or fundraising. It is very important to provide proper documentation and use correct wording and procedures when requesting funding. Initial requests for funding are frequently turned down, but appeals can be successful.

KEY POINTS

- Parents and students have the right to information that is specific to their child's needs.

- Parents and students have the right to expect help from schools and agencies.

- Students have the right to get needed technology.

- Parents and students have the right to honest answers from others about students' technology needs.

- Students have the right to be as independent as possible.

- Parents and students have the right to due process.

- Parents and students have the right to their own opinions and to disagree with others.

A CHILD'S SITUATION TO CONSIDER: TED

Ted is an active four-year-old who lives in a small rural community with his parents and younger sisters. He has been attending preschool special education classes. Ted has normal mental capabilities, but his mild cerebral palsy makes his speech very difficult to understand. Because of the speech therapy he has received, Ted is able to make some speech sounds but he says no words that can be understood by others. He uses sign to communicate with his special education teacher and his parents. Since no one else in his community uses sign, Ted is limited in his ability to communicate with others.

As Ted's IEP Team looks ahead to his entry into elementary school, the Team recognizes that he will need better communication methods in order to participate successfully in the regular classroom. His speech therapist has recommended that Ted begin to use an AlphaTalker.

- *What funding sources might pay for the AlphaTalker?*
- *What case could you make for funding? Are there any obstacles to seeking funding?*

Ted's Solution

At this point Ted's ability to communicate is somewhat limited. Because of his cerebral palsy, Ted is not able to use conventional sign so the gestures he makes are understood only by those who know him well. A simple electronic communication device may work for Ted but there are some prerequisite communication skills he will have to master first. Augmentative communication devices operate on the principle of choosing icons (pictorial symbols) that represent certain basic communications like a cup to indicate "I want a drink."

In order to make a picture/symbol system meaningful and functional for Ted at his young age, his speech therapist began to work on point-to-object and point-to-picture activities. When Ted had mastered point-to-picture activities, his therapist made a picture ring for him. On the ring were picture symbols (icons) for things that Ted might want to say. Ted's family, his teacher, and his classmates began to ask him to use his pictures to explain what he wanted. Soon Ted was using pictures to communicate simple wants and needs effectively. His word ring went with him everywhere and helped him to communicate with people he did not know as well as with friends and family members.

An unexpected bonus to the picture practice is that Ted is verbalizing more and his speech has become more intelligible. He has even begun to sing! An electronic communication device may be in Ted's future, but for now he is learning to communicate well with his picture ring and some spoken word.

Solution Summary

Point-to-picture practice
Use of picture ring

A CHILD'S SITUATION TO CONSIDER: GLORIA

Gloria, an eighteen-year-old with cerebral palsy, is about to finish high school. She has been using a laptop computer and switch access hardware and software in lieu of a pencil and paper to complete work in high school. The equipment and software were provided by the school district through the IEP process. Gloria's current goal, articulated in her Individual Transition Plan (ITP) as mandated by IDEA, is to have a full-time job by the time she is 22. She wants to work in an office and would use a computer system similar to her current setup. As she moves into the transition period, these questions must be addressed:

• *Will the laptop computer she has been using be functional for her in the workplace?*

• *Will she need to consider new equipment? What would influence a decision to purchase new equipment?*

- *What funding sources might help Gloria to purchase new equipment?*

- *What case should Gloria make for funding?*

Gloria's Solution

Gloria is fortunate to have learned computer and word processing skills while she was in school. Now she must learn ways to transfer these skills into the work setting. Laptop computers are not typical in offices; instead, what Gloria is more likely to encounter is a desktop workstation with computer and printer. In order to use a standard computer, Gloria will need a switch access device and an onscreen keyboard to do word processing and data entry.

Since single switch access is necessary for Gloria to become employed in an office setting, Gloria's Vocational Rehabilitation Counselor was willing to make such a purchase for her. Gloria applied to be a data processor with a temporary employment firm and got the job. Gloria's VR counselor helped her to select switch access hardware compatible with most IBM compatible computers. In her new job, Gloria changes office settings frequently. Each time she moves, she takes her switch access device and onscreen keyboard software with her. With these portable items, she is able to adapt each new office setting to meet her needs. Having the right technology has made Gloria an adaptable and successful temporary office employee.

Solution Summary

Switch access
Onscreen keyboard software

CHAPTER 4

Making Assistive Technology Part of a Child's Education

The ideal time for a child with a disability to learn to use assistive technology is when the child is learning all sorts of other skills in early intervention services, preschool, and K-12 education. Children who are eligible for early intervention services or special education [Part B] of the Individuals with Disabilities Education Act (IDEA) are entitled to be evaluated for assistive technology needs and to receive assistive technology devices and services if they are necessary for providing a free, appropriate public education. In order for children to receive the assistive technology to which they are entitled, parents must be knowledgeable about how assistive technology fits into special education and the ways that assistive technology can be included in a child's Individualized Family Service Plan (IFSP) or Individualized Education Program .

ASSISTIVE TECHNOLOGY FOR YOUNG CHILDREN

Parents are often surprised to learn that assistive technology can be appropriate for infants and toddlers. Very young children who have disabilities that limit their ability to interact with the environment by crawling, touching, seeing, or hearing can benefit from technology that improves their interactions. Federal law requires states to "promote the use of assistive technology devices and assistive technology services, where appropriate, to enhance the development of infants and toddlers with disabilities." The law further requires states to "facilitate the transition of infants with disabilities ... from medical care to early intervention services, and the transition from early intervention services to preschool special education or regular education services."

Example: When Kayla was an infant, her interactions with the environment were very limited because she has a genetic condition resulting in abnormally short arms and legs. She could not turn over or crawl; she had difficulty touching and grasping objects. As part of her early intervention program, Kayla was introduced at the age of six months to the use of switches. When the switches were positioned correctly, she could activate switch-operated toys or noisemakers. The opportunity to interact with toys opened up Kayla's world. She soon began to hunt for the switches and to activate certain toys on command. She used the switches to make choices between toys or sounds. She became verbally more expressive and began to interact more readily and more often with her parents and siblings.

By the time that Kayla was three and ready for preschool special education, she was able to sit up and interact with a computer activated by switches. She could identify objects on the computer screen and match those objects to real objects in the world around her. At three, Kayla could identify and match some letters and shapes on the computer screen. Though limited in her mobility, Kayla became an active participant in classroom activities. She could interact with classmates by playing computer games, joining in at circle time, and participating in all preacademic learning activities.

Assistive technology was an integral and necessary part of Kayla's early intervention services. Kayla's parents were involved in writing the Individualized Family Service Plans (IFSPs) that outlined the services Kayla and their family needed. From the beginning, Kayla's family had the opportunity to see how assistive technology could be included in her early special education program and really make a difference in Kayla's education and her life.

Kayla's story illustrates how assistive technology can be utilized from an early age and can be part of the transition from medical treatment to early intervention and from early intervention into preschool special education or regular education. Because of the availability of early intervention services, there is no reason to wait until a child is of school age before trying assistive technology. Early use of the necessary technology will enhance a child's development by increasing opportunities to interact with the environment.

ASSISTIVE TECHNOLOGY AT SCHOOL AGE AND BEYOND

When students enter kindergarten and begin their regular public school years, assistive technology can continue to be a part of their special education programs. For students who are eligible for special education, assistive technology must be provided when it is necessary:

- to support placement in the least restrictive environment,
- to ensure that a student benefits from his or her education, *or*
- to implement the goals and objectives in the student's Individualized Education Program.

Needs for assistive technology should be one of the considerations when a student is assessed to determine eligibility for special education. If an assessment reveals that a student is eligible for special education, then the multi-disciplinary team should consider assistive technology needs when making recommendations for the Individualized Education Program (IEP). The team should analyze what is required of nondisabled students of the same age and determine how many of these requirements could be completely or partially fulfilled by the student being assessed if that student had access to appropriate assistive technology.

In addition, when information is being collected for the present level of performance, describing part of that assessment should be a consideration of whether or not assistive technology is necessary for the student to achieve educational or social goals, benefit from education, or make reasonable progress in the least restrictive educational setting. Whoever is collecting the information might experiment with assistive technology applications to determine which ones might work for the particular student.

Assistive technology should be considered as an option for every Individual Educational Plan. Some students, of course, will not require technology, but many students will benefit from technology. School districts are not required to provide all of the possible assistive devices that might be nice to have or might provide the best possible arrangements. Assistive technology is required, however, when its presence enables the student to make reasonable progress toward the goals the IEP team identifies.

HOW TO INCLUDE ASSISTIVE TECHNOLOGY IN THE CHILD'S INDIVIDUAL EDUCATION PLAN

Assistive technology can be included in the IEP in a number of ways. It may appear as part of the student's annual goals or short term objectives. It may also appear in a list of specific accommodations which need to be made in order for the student to function in the least restrictive environment. For example, the IEP might include such accommodations as the use of word processing, use of a calculator, use of a hand held spell checker and so forth. In addition, the IEP may specify that as a related service necessary for the student to benefit from his or her education, the student will receive training in the use of assistive equipment like an electronic communication device, a power wheelchair, or a personal computer.

Where to Put Assistive Technology in the IEP

There are three places in the IEP where assistive technology may appear: (1) in the annual goals and short term objectives, (2) in the enumeration of supplementary aids and services necessary to maintain the student in the least restrictive educational setting, and (3) in the list of related services necessary for the student to benefit from his or her education.

Assistive technology can be a part of the annual goals and short term objectives on an IEP, but there must be a certain degree of specificity in the goal in order for the role of assistive technology to be clear. An annual goal for the IEP should express an estimate of what the student can accomplish in a particular domain during the course of one year, under what conditions the skill is to be developed, and what criteria will be used to indicate whether or not the skill has been learned.

Many times IEP goals are broad, vague, and totally nonspecific. Such goals are impossible to measure and do not give any indication of what is realistic to expect in terms of the student's behavior or skill level in the course of a year's time. Such broad goals are not useful in addressing assistive technology. The inclusion of assistive technology in the IEP requires a degree of specificity so that it is clear how and why the technology will be used to accomplish a particular goal.

An annual goal which includes assistive technology may indicate that the technology will be part of the conditions under which some academic or social skill will be acquired. For example, an IEP goal for a student with a learning disability in written expression may look like this:

1.0 Using a word processing program with spelling checker, Shawn will compose three paragraph themes composed of fifteen or more sentences with 80% or better accuracy in the use of spelling, punctuation and grammar.

Objectives leading to this goal might include preliminary exploration of the word processing program; trials to learn effective use of the spelling checker; drill and practice in writing single paragraphs to the 80% level of accuracy in spelling, punctuation and grammar; increasing the length of writing to two paragraphs; and then eventually moving to three paragraphs with gradually increasing degrees of accuracy.

Another type of annual goal may address a skill which is necessary for using assistive technology. Such a goal might appear this way:

2.0 Using an adapted computer keyboard, Rachel will type 12 words per minute with no errors over 10 or more consecutive trials.

In this case, Rachel would spend a year learning keyboarding skills with the goal of achieving at least 12 words per minute with complete accuracy. For a young student who experiences some fine motor difficulties, this goal would be challenging but it might be achievable in a year's time. Objectives leading to this goal might involve preliminary exploration of the keyboard, gradual introduction of the letters and numbers on the keyboard, practice to build speed and accuracy, and eventually timed trials until 10 consecutive trials could be achieved with no errors at a rate of 12 words per minute or better.

Still another type of annual goal might address a social issue like communication with peers.

3.0 Using an electronic communication device, Sara will respond appropriately to social inquiries from classmates 5 times out of 5 opportunities over 5 consecutive days.

Objectives leading to this goal might include training in the use of particular words and phrases on the communication device, drill and practice in responding with the device in structured settings, increasing accuracy in responding in structured settings, practice in unstructured conversational opportunities, and gradual achievement of accuracy in unstructured conversational settings with peers.

ASSISTIVE TECHNOLOGY AS A RELATED SERVICE

Assistive technology can be a related service just like audiology, physical therapy, or speech therapy if it is necessary for the student to benefit from his or her education. For a student to be successful in using assistive technology, he or she must be trained in its use. Training to use a computer, an augmentative communication device, a Phonic Ear, or large type viewer or other similar devices can occur as a related service which supports the student's educational program. Preparation for the use of assistive technology can also be worked into other related services like occupational therapy. Occupational therapy may involve determining correct positioning to take advantage of assistive technology and exercises to prepare the student to use a computer keyboard or a communication board.

Example: Margo, who has muscular dystrophy, uses a laptop computer every day in her sixth grade class. Margo's upper body strength is diminishing, and she is gradually having greater and greater difficulty using her hands for writing or drawing. Using a computer saves her energy and allows her to keep performing well in the classroom. As a related service in her IEP, Margo is receiving occupational therapy designed to prepare her for even more adaptations which may be necessary as she loses more strength. Margo and her therapist are experimenting with computer access devices (e.g., switches, trackball) and on screen keyboards to determine what method Margo would like to use when her hands are no longer strong enough to type on a standard keyboard. This special training for assistive technology is written into Margo's IEP as a related service because such training is necessary for her to continue to benefit from her education.

Assistive Technology Support for Placement in the Least Restrictive Environment

One important feature of assistive technology is the fact that it can make it easier for students with and without disabilities to learn together. Students with disabilities are guaranteed the right to be with nondisabled peers and to receive their education in the setting which is the least restrictive environment. In order to be successful in the least restrictive environment, students are to be afforded whatever supplementary aids and services are necessary. Among the supplementary aids which may allow a student to remain in a less restrictive environment are a variety of assistive devices that allow the student to perform educational and social tasks. Assistive technology is necessary as a supplementary aid if its presence (along with other necessary aids) supports the student sufficiently to maintain the placement, and its absence requires the student's removal to a more restrictive setting. For example, if a student with multiple physical disabilities can make progress on his or her IEP goals in the regular classroom with the use of a computer and an augmentative communication device and cannot make such progress in that setting without the devices, then those devices are necessary supplementary aids.

Example: Lyle, a fourth grader with cerebral palsy, is a good example of a student who thrives in the regular classroom if he has the use of appropriate technology. Lyle is able to keep up academically with his classmates if he has access to a computer with an adapted keyboard and word prediction software. Lyle has learned to type well and is able to do written assignments in approximately the same amount of time as other students in his class. Without a computer, Lyle could not keep up at all. Handwriting is a laborious task for Lyle and his written product tends to be messy and barely readable. If he could not use a computer, Lyle would have to rely on others to do handwriting for him or he would have to do alternative assignments that require no writing.

Lyle likes being a regular fourth grader. He is proud of his writing on the computer because he is using his own words and learning to edit out his mistakes by himself. With his computer, he does not need the services of an aide and can be completely independent in doing his school work.

Assistive technology in the form of a computer with appropriate software and keyboard adaptations is necessary for Lyle to remain in the regular classroom, working independently. This use of the computer can be written into his IEP as a supplementary aid which is necessary to support Lyle's placement in the least restrictive environment.

Does assistive technology include access to school buildings?

Assistive technology certainly can mean devices that provide access to school buildings and facilities. One important part of a free, appropriate, public education is that students with disabilities are able to get to school, get into the school, and use the school building and facilities. Assistive technology can be used to provide access to the school bus, classroom, playground, gymnasium, auditorium, lunchroom or the equipment in them. Any or all of these needs can be addressed in the IEP.

Bus modifications for improved access and appropriate seating can help with transportation to and from school and school activities. Doors, walkways, handles, switches, stairs, steps, can be modified so that a student with disabilities can use them as effectively as classmates. Appropriate seating and playground modifications can help include students who have disabilities at classroom, lunchroom and recess times.

When an individual graduates from public school, is it still possible to have assistive technology?

If individuals benefit from the use of assistive technology during their school years, the likelihood is that assistive technology will be even more important for them in adult living. Assistive technology can certainly be part of an individual's future after high school, but it is necessary to begin planning for the transition from high school so that the technology and other necessary services are available when needed.

The earlier a family can estimate their child's post-high school needs, including needs for technology, the earlier transition planning can begin. Federal legislation says that transition planning can begin in school as early as "14 or younger." Each student with a disability who has an Individualized Education Program (IEP) should have a "statement of transition services ... beginning no later than age 16." This means that as early as middle school, but probably not later than freshman year in high school, families should begin transition planning.

Unlike school services, services in the adult world are not mandated. An individual may be eligible for a service, but not receive it because all of the slots are filled or funding is not available. If an individual does not own his or her own assistive technology devices, then part of transition planning will be looking into funding sources that could help with technology purchases. If technology is necessary for the person to become employed, it is possible that Vocational Rehabilitation will pay for the devices as part of an Individual Work-Related Plan (IWRP). Students who go on to postsecondary education at community college, vocational-technical schools or universities can expect to be able to receive certain accommodations for their disabilities while on campus. Most postsecondary institutions have Student Support Services that help with assistive technology needs, alternative testing, and personal assistants such as readers and notetakers.

SUMMARY

Assistive technology can be included as an integral part of a student's education, but parents have to be knowledgeable about how to go about getting assistive technology into their children's educational plans. Assistive technology can be written into the Individualized Family Service Plan (IFSP) for infants and toddlers in early intervention programs and into the Individualized Education Program (IEP) for preschoolers and students in grades K through 12. Assistive technology can appear in three places in the IEP: (a) as part of the goals and objectives, (b) as a supplementary aid to support placement in the least restrictive environment, and (c) as a related service. Assistive technology can also be a part of students' transition planning as they move from high school into adult pursuits. Assistive technology is available through Vocational Rehabilitation and other adult disability services, but these services are not mandated. To ensure continued use of assistive technology, it is important to plan ahead and secure funding for devices needed in the work or postsecondary education environments.

HINTS FOR PARENTS

If your child is a successful assistive technology user, begin to save money early in your child's life—just as you might save for college. Gradually accumulate enough funding to purchase the kinds of technology your child will need as an adult. Technology changes so fast that it is impossible to predict what will be available fifteen years from now. But a parent can be certain that assistive technology of the future will be even better than what is available today.

A CHILD'S SITUATION TO CONSIDER: EMILY

Emily is a seventh-grade student who has learning disabilities. She is in regular classes all day in her neighborhood middle school. A special education teacher monitors Emily's progress and provides the regular classroom teachers with assistance by modifying some of Emily's assignments, giving her oral tests, helping to organize Emily's work, and reteaching certain skills, as necessary.

In elementary school, Emily did well with the limited amount of support she received in the regular classroom. In middle school, however, she is having trouble keeping up with assignments. Emily's spelling is inaccurate; she often misspells the same word three or four different ways on the same page. Her handwriting is very slow and laborious so she spends many hours each evening working on her homework. She has tried tape recording assignments, but she finds this process also to be laborious because it is so time consuming to correct mistakes.

It has been recommended that Emily be removed from some of her academic classes and receive instruction in the resource program. Emily wants to remain in regular classes, but she can't keep up with the pace.

- *How could assistive technology help Emily?*
- *What are her needs?*
- *What case could be made for assistive technology for her?*

Emily's Solution

Emily has reached the point in her educational career when she cannot keep pace with the demands of the written work. On observing Emily, the occupational therapist noted that it took Emily five times as long as the average student in her English class to complete written assignments.

Emily's IEP Team decided she was spending far too much time on the handwriting process. To help her with this problem, the team agreed that Emily should learn to use a computer with a word processing program and a voiced spell checker. One period per day, Emily goes to the resource room to practice keyboarding and work on longer written assignments. During her regular classes, Emily uses a portable word processor (e.g., AlphaSmart) to take notes which she can print out later in the resource room.

These simple solutions allow Emily to speed up her writing time and produce written work that is easy to correct and edit. With technology to aid her, Emily is spending less time on the handwriting process and more time on thinking and processing information. Her homework time has been cut in half and Emily is much more relaxed and confident at school.

Solution Summary

Keyboarding training
Use of computer with word processing software
Use of voiced spell checker
Use of portable word processor

A CHILD'S SITUATION TO CONSIDER: BRYAN

Bryan is a seventh grader with a neuromuscular disease that has caused him to lose physical function. He is a bright student with excellent academic skills. Bryan uses a laptop computer with a trackball and an onscreen keyboard to do all his written work. He navigates skillfully around the school building using a power wheelchair. Technology has really helped Bryan to fit in and do well at school. However, now as a young adolescent, Bryan is beginning to feel left out socially. He requires so much help with his physical needs that he has to spend lots of time with adults. Bryan wants to "hang out" like the other kids his age and escape adult scrutiny once in a while.

Bryan does not speak. He uses a complex, sophisticated electronic communication device to participate in class. The device is programmed with phrases that Bryan frequently uses and he also can select icons to create sentences of his own. Bryan's communication device works well for him in formal, classroom settings but it is bulky and cumbersome to use in casual conversation with friends. Bryan has come to believe that his communication device is actually a barrier to the kinds of informal interactions he wants to have.

Bryan knows that he has the best in technology and that the equipment he uses is very expensive. He doesn't want to appear "greedy" or demanding, so he has not told his parents about his dissatisfaction with his ability to communicate. One of Bryan's friends, Michael, however, noticed that Bryan was acting pensive and unusually quiet. Michael gently coaxed the truth out of Bryan and offered to help his friend think of a new way to "talk" that would provide him with more flexibility and independence.

Bryan's Solution

When Bryan and Michael put their heads together, they came up with lots of ideas. The one they settled on as the most feasible involved using the laptop that Bryan already had. The laptop had some advantages because it was small and portable and Bryan already knew how to use it very well. In a catalog of special software, the friends found communication software that operated on an icon system and the price was right--around $100. With communication software installed on the laptop, Bryan had a simpler, more portable device for talking in casual settings.

Next Michael asked his father to help them make a tray for

Bryan's wheelchair that would hold the laptop and fold down beside the chair out of the way when not in use. Michael's dad came up with a clever tray on hinges that folded to the side. The laptop fastened to the tray with wide rubber bands. A handle on the tray allowed Bryan to raise and lower the tray as needed.

In addition to his laptop, Bryan also needed a device for quick greetings and spontaneous retorts. Bryan and Michael chose a programmable switch with the capacity to record up to 12 messages. Bryan could operate the switch quickly by hitting it with his elbow. He and Michael had a great time recording messages suitable for talking to their friends or to girls.

What Bryan found out was that he needed multiple ways to communicate so that he could customize his electronic speech to fit the setting and the occasion. For a relatively small financial investment, Bryan and Michael were able to expand communication possibilities for Bryan and allow him greater control and personal choice about what he said, how he said it, and to whom.

Solution Summary

> Communication software
> Drop-down wheelchair tray
> Programmable switch

AN ADULT'S SITUATION TO CONSIDER: TRACY

Tracy is a man in his mid-thirties who has been blind from birth. Since graduating from college, he has held a series of entry level jobs at minimum wage and without benefits. Tracy is frustrated by the lack of challenge in the jobs he has had; he would like to have a managerial position with some opportunities for advancement, better pay, and benefits.

Currently Tracy is working at a Pizza Hut restaurant where he prepares pizzas for the oven. He enjoys his co-workers and regular customers, but Tracy wants more. A management trainee opening has been announced in the company newsletter and Tracy decides to apply. This new position involves taking pizza orders over the telephone and sending the order via computer and modem to the appropriate Pizza Hut outlet where the pizzas will be made. Having made every possible type and size of pizza, Tracy is very familiar with the options. But how could he operate the computer and record orders as they come in over the telephone? Would he have a chance for this job which could be his first step up?

Tracy's Solution

Tracy and his Vocational Rehabilitation Counselor filled out the job application for the position at Pizza Hut's central ordering facility and Tracy was called to set up an interview. Prior to the interview, Tracy and his job counselor went to the central ordering facility for Pizza Hut to study aspects of the job and to determine if technology could assist Tracy to perform the essential job functions. The job involved the following steps: (1) greeting the customer and taking down customer information, (2) asking a series of questions about the customer's order (e.g., type, size, toppings), (3) simultaneous recording of the order via computer, and (4) sending the order to the appropriate Pizza Hut outlet.

After studying the process of taking orders, Tracy and his counselor decided upon the following technology:

(a) A computer compatible with the Pizza Hut network;

(b) Voiced software so that Tracy could "hear" what he was typing;

(c) A telephone headset to listen to the customer with one ear;

(d) an ear piece to listen to the computer.

At his interview for the job, Tracy explained his qualifications for the position--college degree, experience with Pizza Hut. He also told the interview team about how technology would allow him to do the job as efficiently and effectively as other workers.

The interview team members were impressed by Tracy's initiative and his work ethic. They chose him over several other qualified candidates. Though it took some detective work to put together a computer/software package compatible with Pizza Hut's system, Tracy was able to do it.

From the first day on the job, Tracy knew he was going to like it better than anything he had done before. Listening to the computer and the customer simultaneously was challenging at first, but soon Tracy had mastered the process. After three months in his new position, Tracy was asked to become the manager for his shift. Now he hires and trains new order clerks, schedules workers and evaluates their job performance. Tracy has achieved what he wanted: a managerial position, better wages, and a future with the company.

Solution Summary

Compatible computer terminal
Voiced software
Telephone headset
Ear piece for computer

CHAPTER 5

Advocating for Assistive Technology

In the area of Assistive Technology—just as in so many areas of need—parents must be their children's best advocates. Federal and state laws support providing assistive technology to children with disabilities,but these laws are only meaningful when parents know about them and can use legal processes to secure their children's rights.

FEDERAL LAW ON ASSISTIVE TECHNOLOGY

Here are just a few of the laws on which parents can rely when advocating for assistive technology for their children:

The Americans with Disabilities Act of 1990

The 1990 Americans with Disabilities Act (ADA) proposes to elimi-nate "... discrimination against individuals with disabilities ... to address the major areas of discrimination faced day-to-day by people with disabilities." The ADA applies specifically to the areas of em-ployment, public accommodations, and government functions. In these areas, the ADA requires that reasonable accommodations be made so that people with disabilities can have an equal opportu-nity to participate in employment opportunities, public accom-modations, and government functions. The ADA's definition of "auxiliary aids and services," its mandates for "acquisition or modifications of equipment and devices" and "reasonable accommodations" support the provision of assistive technology devices and services to individuals with disabilities.

The Rehabilitation Act of 1973

Section 504 of the rehabilitation Act requires that any "program or activity receiving Federal financial assistance" comply with nondiscrimination rules. Section 504 regulations require that public schools provide students who have disabilities an educational opportunity equal to the educational opportunity provided to students without disabilities. Section 504 also uses the term "reasonable accommodations" which can mean the provision of assistive technology devices and services.

The Individuals with Disabilities Education Act (IDEA)

The Individuals with Disabilities Education Act (IDEA) requires free, appropriate, public education (FAPE) for students with disabilities. IDEA mandates education in the least restrictive environment, requires schools to use supplementary aids and services and special and related services to help assure that students with disabilities participate in and benefit from public education. Assistive technology is specifically mentioned in IDEA as a service which school districts may have to provide in order for a student with disabilities to benefit from special education.

The Carl Perkins Act

The Carl Perkins Act assures that Vocational Education programs in public schools are made accessible to students with disabilities. The law assures supplementary services including classroom, curriculum and equipment modifications, supportive personnel, instructional aides and instructional devices.

PARENT RESPONSIBILITIES

In order to be effective advocates for their children, parents need to familiarize themselves with all the laws that support the provision of assistive technology. Copies of the laws and their regulations are available from the offices of members of the House of Representatives and the Senate. Besides knowing the law, parents must participate actively in developing plans for their children's education that include assistive technology, when it is needed. Parents must attend IFSP and IEP meetings and be prepared to work cooperatively with other team members. When a parent questions an assistive technology evaluation or an IEP Team recommendation, the parent must be prepared to follow-up on those questions, including using due process procedure when necessary.

What should a parent do when an agency refuses to pay for assistive technology that a child needs?

Agencies like early intervention programs and school districts are mandated to provide assistive technology if the need for technology is in the child's written plan. If one of these agencies refuses to pay for needed technology, then a parent must consider exercising due process rights. In early intervention services, the parent would follow the appeal process laid out by the lead agency. When school district services are involved, the parent can file a complaint if services in the IEP are not provided or can ask for a due process hearing if the parent and the school district disagree about the need for assistive technology. If a parent disagrees with the results of an evaluation for assistive technology, the parent can ask for an independent evaluation at school district expense. Parents may get more information and assistance from the closest Parent Training and Information Center or from the state's Protection and Advocacy Office. (See the Resources section at the back of this book.)

SUMMARY

Overall, getting the devices and services for children with disabilities means that parents must be part of the planning team at every level of their child education. It means talking with other families and users of assistive technology about devices and services, learning how they found the best technology, and figuring out where to go when resources are few. Getting assistive devices and services is not always an easy job. But help is available. Working with professionals, talking with consumers and other families, parents can find the best avenues for providing their children with the assistive technology they need. In the end the effort is worth it because assistive technology is not just a civil right guaranteed by law; it is also a means to achieve human rights to grow up happy, independent and as self-sufficient as possible.

KEY POINTS

- Advocacy helps to protect a student's rights and to obtain needed technology.

- Parents should get information about a student in order to be good advocates.

- Communication skills are important when talking with professionals.

- Parents should keep records of all the things they do to get technology.

- Parents should ask questions whenever they don't fully understand something.

- Parents should avoid traps in communicating with professionals.

- Follow-up is important.
- Parents can appeal the decision of the IEP committee.

HINTS FOR PARENTS

When advocating for your child in the special education arena, don't forget the following facts about assistive technology and the IEP:

- Assistive technology needs must be considered along with a student's other educational needs.
- Needs for technology must be identified on an individual basis.
- Identification of technology needs must involve parents, the student when appropriate, and a multidisciplinary team.
- Parents or other IEP Team members can ask for additional evaluation or an independent evaluation to determine assistive technology needs.
- When an evaluation is being conducted, consider mobility, fine-motor skills, communication, and alternatives to traditional learning approaches.
- Lack of availability of equipment or cost alone cannot be used as an excuse for denying assistive technology services.
- If included in the IEP, assistive technology services and devices must be provided at no cost to the family.
- Parents always have the right to appeal if assistive technology services are denied.

CHAPTER 6

More Questions and Answers

Are schools required to pay for assistive technology devices and services?

It is the responsibility of the school district to provide for the equipment, services or programs identified in the IEP. The school district may pay for the equipment, service or programs itself; utilize other resources to provide or pay for the device; or utilize private insurance funds, Medicaid, or other sources of funds as long as the device or service identified in the IEP is provided at *no cost to the parent.* Private insurance or Medicaid may be used only if the parent agrees.

Can schools require the parents to pay for an assistive technology device or service identified in the student's IEP, or require the parents to use their own private health insurance to pay for the device or service?

No. The "free" in FAPE means that parents of students with disabilities who require assistive technology devices or services do not have to pay for these items. As stated in IDEA and its regulations, all special education and related services identified in the student's IEP must be provided "at no cost to the parent." The term "free" is interpreted broadly and goes far beyond the simple paying of deductibles and co-payments. The courts have interpreted "free" to apply to, but not be limited to, future insurability, depletion of maximum lifetime caps, raised premiums, discontinuation of policies, and preexisting condition exclusions. If the family agrees to allow the school to access their Medicaid or private insurance, this decision must be strictly voluntary on the part of the family.

How can school districts use Medicaid funds to purchase assistive technology devices?

If Medicaid is limited expenditure for an individual in any way concerning its use for assistive devices, school districts must request from parents the right to use Medicaid funds. However, parents are not obligated to use their Medicaid funds to purchase devices or services used at school. With permission, a parent's private insurance must be accessed before Medicaid can be used for assistive technology devices. Medicaid regulations vary somewhat from state to state so it is wise to consult the state Medicaid Service Bureau before making any assumptions about Medicaid and the purchase of assistive technology.

Are there other options for schools to consider in lieu of purchasing the assistive technology device?

Yes. There are times when the outright purchase of equipment or devices is not necessary or even advisable. In such instances, schools might consider rental or long-term lease options. There are certain advantages to renting or leasing, depending on the individual needs of the student. For example, renting equipment might be a reasonable strategy if the student is expected to improve or deteriorate in a short period of time, or when it is necessary to try out the equipment before purchase. Long-term leasing or lease/purchase agreements also have potential benefits for schools which include: no obligation on behalf of the school to purchase the device; ability to return leased equipment and thus reduce obsolete inventory; flexible leasing terms; use of equipment without a lump-sum purchase; upgrading of equipment as more improved technology becomes available; and upgrading of equipment as the student's needs change.

Won't students become too dependent on technology and not learn to use the skills they have?

Assistive technology should be used as support for access, learning and performing daily tasks. In general, assistive technology is appropriate when it compensates for disabilities so that the individual can function as normally as possible. If assistive technology is necessary for a student to have access to educational opportunities or to benefit from education, then it is a legitimate support. Some skills are too laborious or taxing to accomplish at a rate or with degree of proficiency to allow for participation in the least restrictive environment. With assistive technology, the student can participate more fully and more closely approximate the levels of achievement and interaction of his or her peers. In general, the use of assistive technology enhances function and increases skills and opportunities. Though a student may be dependent upon a particular device in order to perform skillfully, denying the device denies the student an opportunity ever to achieve success at the level of his or her potential.

When is assistive technology appropriate?

Assistive technology may be considered appropriate when it does any or all of the following things:

- Enables students to perform functions that can be achieved by no other means

- Enables students to approximate normal fluency, rate, or standards—a level of accomplishment which could not be achieved by any other means

- Provides access for participation in programs or activities which otherwise would be closed to the individual

- Increases endurance or ability to persevere and complete tasks that otherwise are too laborious to be attempted on a routine basis

- Enables students to concentrate on learning tasks, rather than mechanical tasks

- Provides greater access to information

- Supports normal social interactions with peers and adults

- Supports participation in the least restrictive educational enviroment.

Who owns the special equipment that is purchased for students?

If the school district purchases the equipment, the equipment belongs to the district. Some school districts designate that a particular device is to be used by a specific student during the time when that device remains appropriate for that student. Other districts have "pools" of assistive devices and distribute them for use by a variety of students. The distribution and use of devices is under the district's control as long as the needs described in students' IEPs are being met.

If devices are purchased for a particular student using that student's Medicaid funds or private insurance, then the device belongs to the student and is meant for the exclusive use of that student.

When a student moves from one level of schooling to another like elementary school to middle school, does the device follow the student?

If an assistive device is necessary in order to fulfill the requirements of a student's IEP, such a device must be provided in whatever school the student attends. The same device may not necessarily follow the student from one school to another, but a comparable device which fulfills the IEP requirements would have to be provided in the new school that the student attends.

If a family moves from one school district to another, can a student's assistive technology go along?

Devices bought by the school belong to the school, not the student who uses them. When a family moves from one school district to another, the equipment the student has been using does not automatically move to the new school.

Assistive equipment can go with a student to a new school if the sending school district agrees to sell or give the device to the family or the new school district.

If the device was purchased by the family, through the family's private health insurance or by Medicaid for this particular student, then the device belongs to the student and can go with the student to a new school district.

What happens to assistive technology devices when students leave the school system at graduation?

If the school district purchased the device, the device is the property of the school. The school could keep the device for use by other students, sell it or decide to transfer the device to another district or loan program. If the family or another funding source purchased the device, it is the property of the student and the family.

If a piece of assistive technology is no longer needed by a student and the device was paid for by Medicaid or private insurance, can it be donated for another student's benefit?

Yes, it is a parental decision. The parents could donate the device to the school for use by other students with disabilities or to some other organization which loans out equipment.

Can assistive devices be insured?

Many school district liability policies will cover devices purchased by the district for student use. Devices purchased by other funding sources may or may not be covered while on school premises or involved in school activities. It is important for school staff to investigate the district's property insurance to determine what the policy currently covers and whether or not the policy insures against loss or damage of assistive devices.

Parents who own assistive devices that are used at home and at school may also wish to purchase home owners or renters' insurance with a special rider that covers damage to or loss of the device.

Who is responsible for the repair and maintenance of assistive devices?

In general, the school district is responsible for repair and maintenance of assistive devices used to support educational programs described in the IEP or covered by Section 504.

If a device is broken and is beyond repair, who replaces the broken device?

If an assistive device is necessary for the student's IEP to be implemented, then the school district will have to replace a broken, lost, or stolen device.

If a device is broken and sent off for repairs, must the school district supply a substitute device until the original device is returned?

If the assistive technology device is vital to the student's daily special education program, it is not reasonable for the student to be without a device for long periods of time. If a device is going to be unavailable for more than a day or two, the district should provide a backup machine which allows the student to continue working on IEP goals.

Is the school district obligated to train substitute teachers and aides to operate assistive technology devices?

Again, if the assistive technology device is vital to the student's daily special education program, it is not reasonable for the student not to be able to use the device for long periods of time because a substitute is teaching the class. If the substitute is only going to be in the classroom for a day or two, it is probably not necessary to provide elaborate training. However, if the substitute is going to be in the classroom for an extended time, training should be provided.

Must school districts allow students to take assistive devices home on school nights to do homework? Over weekends? During school vacations? Over the summer?

In many cases, it is desirable for students to have the opportunity to use the same assistive technology devices at home and in school. For example, when a student is completing homework assignments, assistive technology may be necessary to produce the type of product that is required. Some school districts have policies which allow the devices to go home with the students overnight, on weekends, or during vacation or summer periods. In general, these kinds of policies are a local district matter and may be determined according to local district needs. If, however, a student's IEP includes a provision which says the student is to have access to an assistive device both at school and at home, then the school district would be obligated to allow the student to take a device home or provide two devices, one for home use and one for school.

What professionals are considered qualified to assess a student in the area of assistive technology?

Because assistive technology is such a new field, there are no national standards and few local or state standards for licensing or certification for specialists in assistive technology. However, school districts often have professionals who have received training in conducting assistive technology evaluations and are able to provide the services identified in the IEP. If a district does not have personnel who are knowledgeable in conducting such evaluations, the district can arrange for such services from other knowledgeable providers, such as Independent Living Projects, Alliance for Technology Access Centers, or Tech Act Projects (see Appendix).

How can one distinguish between assistive technology and personal items (e.g., wheelchairs, hearing aids, eyeglasses, crutches)?

Currently, IDEA does not make a clear distinction between assistive technology devices and personal items. This confusion stems in large part from IDEAs broad definition of assistive technology. For example, if a student with a disability needs eye glasses in order to obtain FAPE, then the school district is obligated to provide them at no cost to the parents. In general, however, school districts do not purchase personally prescribed devices such as hearing aids or glasses.

Who determines how assistive technology will be purchased and with what available funding resources—the IEP Team or school administration?

Once the IEP team makes the determination that assistive technology must be provided as part of the student's IEP, it is the responsibility of school administration to determine how the assistive technology will be provided and with which funding sources.

Is a school district responsible for providing "state of the art" equipment for a student?

No. The school district need provide only *appropriate* technology in order to meet the student's needs as described in the childs Individual Education Plan (IEP). The decision as to what type of assistive technology is appropriate should be based on the assistive technology evaluation recommendations and IEP team decision. There may be "devices" or features of equipment which may be nice for the student to have, but if they are not necessary for a free appropriate public Education, the school district is not obligated to provide them. If a specific device is necessary to ensure a free appropriate public education (FAPE) and no other device can meet the student's needs, then the district must provide the required device, even though it is costly. If a less expensive device would accomplish the same goals, the IEP team is under no obligation to choose a more expensive option.

If a student needs a computer, can a school-owned computer be used in the lab or classroom?

Yes, a school owned computer can be used if the student has access to the equipment when he or she needs it. If the student does not have the necessary access, then the appropriate equipment should be purchased for the student's use.

Can school district administrators instruct personnel not to include costly assistive technology devices in the IEP?

IEP teams are charged with the responsibility for determining a student's need for assistive technology devices and services, and for specifying those devices and services. Therefore, it is important that IEP teams are clearly informed of their responsibility to determine if a student needs a device and the need for an assistive technology evaluation to assist in making the determination. A school district may not have a policy which prevents IEP teams from identifying a student's need for assistive devices or services.

How does assistive technology get integrated into the curriculum?

The IEP team needs to discuss how the device will be used by the student and how it will be integrated into the curriculum. The IEP team should identify on the IEP how the device will be used by the student in the classroom. This information should be shared with the general classroom teachers so that they are aware of how it is to be used.

How can assistive technology be provided from year to year with a degree of continuity?

As part of the annual review of the IEP, a point should be made to devise ways to communicate with next year's teachers about the technology the student uses and how it should be integrated into the curriculum. Teachers who are new to working with the student who uses technology should be provided training if they are unfamiliar with the device and its use. Training for teachers and support staff should be written into the IEP as a related service.

Can an assistive technology device be used by more than one student?

Yes, if the device is the property of the school district and if all of the students using the device have access to the equipment when they need it.

Can an independent evaluation be requested to address assistive technology?

Yes. The school district is required to evaluate a student in all areas of suspected disability, including, if appropriate, evaluating the student's need for assistive technology. A parent has the right to an independent educational evaluation at public expense if the parent disagrees with an evaluation obtained by the school district. However, the school district may initiate a due process hearing to show that its evaluation is appropriate. If the final decision is that the evaluation is appropriate, the parent still has the right to an independent educational evaluation, but not at public expense. If the parent obtains an independent educational evaluation at private expense, the results of the evaluation (a) must be considered by the school district in any decision made with respect to the provision of FAPE to the child; and (b) may be presented as evidence at a due process hearing.

What is a product system?

A product system is more than one piece of equipment working together to produce a result. For example, an FM system that works in conjunction with a student's hearing aid is a product system.

Can the school district require a student to bring a personally owned assistive device, such as an augmentative communication system or laptop computer to school in order to do schoolwork?

No. However, the family may wish the child to use his or her equipment in school since the child may be more familiar or comfortable with it. The IEP team should decide who is responsible for repair and maintenance of family owned devices.

Is it sufficient for a school district to supply access to a district-owned computer, but provide no software that is appropriate for the student to use?

Just providing access to a computer does not fulfill the district's obligation to provide assistive technology to support FAPE. The educational aspect of the computer is very much related to the software that the student uses. If no appropriate software is available, then the student cannot pursue the IEP goals.

QUESTIONS TO ASK ABOUT TECHNOLOGY

If the item has been considered, place a check mark next to the item.

___ What are my child's needs?

___ What are my child's (or my own) preferences for technology?

___ Is the device gender-appropriate (what a boy/girl would use)?

___ Is the technology right for my child's age?

___ Have my child's home and family activities been considered?

___ What are the transportation needs for my child?

___ What are my child's wishes for a future job?

___ Will the school pay for the technology my child needs?

___ Am I able to pay for the device that my child needs?

___ How can technology help my child meet his or her educational goals?

___ How many different types of devices can meet my child's needs?

___ Does the technology do what it is supposed to do?

___ How much will the device really cost?

___ Can my child comfortably operate the technology?

___ Is the device dependable?

__ Can the technology be moved easily?

__ How long is the device likely to last?

__ Can the technology be used with other devices?

__ Will my child be able to try the device before it is bought?

__ How easy is it to take care of the technology from day to day?

__ How secure is the device?

__ How easy is the technology to put together?

__ How easy is it to get the technology repaired?

CHECKLIST FOR ADVOCACY ACTIVITIES

If the item has been considered, place a check mark next to the item.

Understanding the Problem

__ What are the needs that my child has because of the disability?

__ How does my child feel about the needs?

__ Is the need one that has been present for a long time? Or is the need one which only occurs at certain times?

__ What are solutions to address the need? What agencies or people might help me address the needs?

__ What has already been done to meet my child's needs?

__ What has the school done to help meet my child's needs?

Gathering Information

__ Have I called people in the community to find out who provides services that my child needs?

__ Do I have copies of documents from community agencies that discuss my child's rights and services provided?

__ Do I have information about the chain of command in community agencies that might help my child?

__ Do I have information about the laws that affect my child?

__ Do I have copies of tests and reports about my child?

__ Have I reviewed my child's case files?

__ Have I kept notes of people's names and what they have said as I have made calls to people who work for agencies?.

Putting Suggestions Into Action

__ Have I written down how to get needed technology for my child?

__ Do my communication skills need to be improved?

These include:

- keeping eye contact with people when talking to them;
- keeping good body posture when talking with people;
- using facial and body expressions when talking with people;
- controlling the tone of my voice when talking with people;
- letting people know that I understand what they are saying; and
- asking questions.

Taking Action

__ Have I suggested to professionals that the meeting to discuss my child's technology needs take place in my home?

__ Have I suggested that the meeting to discuss my child's technology needs take place in a church, library, or public building?

__ Have I made myself familiar with the meeting place?

__ Can I get to the meeting place early?

__ Have I looked at the seating arrangements for the meeting?

__ Do I know who will be at the meeting and what their roles are?

__ Will other family members or friends be with me at the meeting?

__ Have I made a list of things to discuss with the people present at the meeting? Are the most difficult issues listed first or last?

___ Have the people at the meeting agreed on the meeting length?

___ If I become upset at the meeting, will I be able to ask for more information or ask for a short break?

___ If words are used at the meeting that I don't understand, will I be able to ask people to explain what they mean?

___ Can I keep from telling people that they have to do something?

ASSISTIVE TECHNOLOGY: any sort of aid, including computers, switches, calculators, spelling devices, communication devices and voice synthesizers, which is used to help an individual perform some task of daily living.

ALTERNATIVE KEYBOARD: may include enlarged, reduced, varied key placement, one-handed, braille, chordic, or any other device for entering text on a computer.

AUGMENTATIVE COMMUNICATION: any device (electronic or otherwise) to enhance communication for a person with limited speech.

BRAILLE EMBOSSER: a printer for producing braille output either manually or when connected to a computer. When printing standard text from a computer, it must first be translated into braille.

BRANCHING: describes the process of choosing among a sequence of choices or actions to produce another sequence of choices. This process is used in the "scanning" method of access.

CD-ROM: "Compact Disk Read-Only Memory" refers to the 4-inch silver disks that typically hold 700 megabytes of digital information and the players that access the information on these disks.

CURSOR: either the flashing vertical or horizontal line on a computer screen that indicates the insertion point for text; or the arrow or I-beam that indicates the position of the mouse pointer on the computer screen.

DESK ACCESSORY: a small utility program that runs on a computer and may be accessed from any program at any time (such as a calculator).

DRILL AND PRACTICE: presents questions repetitively, but is not a tutorial. Software that is only drill and practice doesn't necessarily teach the concepts needed to answer the questions presented.

ENVIRONMENTAL CONTROL: any type of device that an individual may use to control the environment (lights, appliances, TV, telephone, etc). This may include anything from simple reachers or sticks to computers and voice-activated electronic systems.

FAPE: the free, appropriate public education required for all students with special needs under the Federal Statutes.

FM SYSTEM: a local wireless broadcast system that consists of a microphone and transmitter for the speaker and "walkman-like" receivers with headphones for listeners with hearing impairments or attention disorders.

HIGH TECH: use of electronics or computers as a solution.

ICON: a small computer graphic that appears on the computer screen and may represent different types of objects (files or applications) or actions, depending on the context. Use the mouse pointer to click on icons that open files or perform other actions.

INDIVIDUAL FAMILY SERVICE PLAN (IFSP): the written document which defines the early intervention services provided to the child and family. The program is designed to meet the needs of the child and the family, and is based on family-identified priorities.

INDIVIDUALIZED EDUCATION PROGRAM (IEP): a written plan, specifying instructional goals and any special education and related services a student may need, which must be written and reviewed annually. Included are (1) the present educational levels of the student; (2) a statement of annual goals, including short-term objectives; (3) a statement of specific services, if needed; (4) the programs; (5) the date when special services are to begin and the expected duration of these services; and (6) the tests and other requirements or information used to gauge the student's progress to determine if the instructional objectives are being met.

INPUT: the information that is transmitted to a computer from a keyboard, mouse or other input device.

KEYBOARD: a device for inputting text and commands to a computer.

KEYGUARD: a plexiglass or other cover for a keyboard with holes for the individual keys. It allows more precise selection of keys for an individual with fine motor difficulties.

KEYPAD: a small keyboard with a 10-key setup for numeric input, or it may also be used as a control for a screen-reader program.

LAPTOP: a portable battery-powered computer that is typically the size of a 3-ring binder, weighs 5-10 pounds, and consists of a screen, keyboard and disk-drives.

LASER DISCS: large (12-inch) CD-ROMs that normally contain movies.

LOW TECH: indicates use of low cost non-electronic solutions.

MACRO: a simple short program that performs an action on a computer. A macro is usually created by recording the keyboard and/or mouse input and storing it as an icon or key combination.

MEGABYTE: 1,000 X 2^{10} bytes of information, which basically means over one million keystrokes of computer storage (about 10 novels).

MORSE CODE: a direct method for computer input using one to three switches and coded input to replace the keyboard and mouse.

MOUSE: the name given to the pointing device used to control graphical user interfaces (GUI) of modern personal computers.

ONSCREEN KEYBOARD: a software program that places the keyboard on the screen of the computer and may be accessed using a mouse or other pointing device. This is ideal for individuals who cannot use a regular keyboard, but can use some type of pointing device.

OPTICAL CHARACTER RECOGNITION (OCR): a process that utilizes special computer software to convert the scanned image of text into actual text that may be edited by a word processor.

OUTPUT: computer-generated information for the user. This may be printed output from a printer, visual information from the screen, or sounds from speakers.

SCANNER: an electronic copier connected to a computer. Scanners are used to input drawings, pictures or printed text into the computer.

SCANNING: has nothing to do with the electronic copier above. It is another method for accessing a computer or communication device using one or more switches. Scanning involves presenting a group of choices, cycling among them and making choices by activating a switch.

SCREEN READER: software that reads text on a computer screen using a speech synthesizer. This allows individuals with visual or other print disabilities to access text on the computer screen.

SIMULATION: software that simulates real-world situations on a computer. This may range from a joystick trainer for driving an electric wheelchair to running cities.

SPEECH SYNTHESIZER: hardware or software for producing electronic human speech on a computer.

SPELL CHECKER: utility for checking the spelling in a document.

STICKY KEYS: software or mechanical utility for allowing typing of multiple keystrokes with one finger (using the shift or other modifier keys).

SWITCH: a device that is like a single button of a keyboard or mouse. Switches may be used by an individual with severe motor difficulties by any controllable muscle in the body (head, hand, toe, eye, breath, etc.) to operate any type of computer, communication or environmental control device.

SWITCH INTERFACE: black box that connects to a computer or other device that has plugs for switches.

TDD: a text telephone used for communicating in typed text over a phone line. A TDD has a keyboard and text display or small printer. Both parties who are communicating over a phone line must have TDDs.

TOUCH WINDOW: a computer input device that uses a touch-sensitive transparent window placed on the computer screen. It performs mouse functions with a finger or stylus directly on the screen.

TRACKBALL: another replacement for the mouse pointing device that uses a rolling ball to perform mouse movements.

TUTORIAL: teaches concepts, presents information as opposed to simple drill and practice.

VOICE RECOGNITION: computer software and microphone that allows input and control with voice commands.

WORD PREDICTION: productivity software that increases typing speed for one-finger typists and others by predicting and choosing complete words.

WORD PROCESSOR: software for inputting and formatting text.

USER: person using a computer.

UTILITY: software for adding function or performing housekeeping tasks on a computer.

RESOURCES

Parent Training and Information Centers

ALABAMA

Special Education Action Committee, Inc. (SEAC)
3207 International Dr., Ste. C
PO Box 161274
  Mobile AL 36616-2274
334-478-1208
800-222-7322 (AL only)
334-473-7877 (fax)

ALASKA

Alaska PARENTS Inc.
540 International Airport Rd Ste 200
Anchorage AK 99518
907-563-2246
800-478-7678 (AK only)
907-563-2257 (fax)
parents@corcom.com
http://www.corcom.com/parents

AMERICAN SAMOA

American Samoa Parent Network
PO Box 3432
Pago Pago AS 96799
684-633-2407
684-633-7707 (fax)

ARIZONA

Pilot Parent Partnerships
4750 N Black Canyon Hwy #101
Phoenix AZ 85017-3621
602-242-4366
800-237-3007 (AZ only)
602-242-4306 (fax)

ARKANSAS

Arkansas Parent Support and Information Network
Arkansas Disability Coalition
3920 Woodland Heights Road
Little Rock AR 72212
501-221-1330
800-223-1330 (AR only)
501-221-9067 (fax)
adc@cei.net

Arkansas Parent Support and Information Network
FOCUS, Inc.
305 W Jefferson Ave
Jonesboro AR 72401
501-931-3755
501-221-1330
501-972-1616 (fax)
10202.2352@compuserve.com

CALIFORNIA

DREDF
2212 Sixth Street
Berkeley CA 94710
510-644-2555
510-841-8645 (fax)
DREDFCA@aolcom

Exceptional Parents Unlimited (EPU)
4120 N First Street
Fresno CA 93726

209-229-2000
209-229-2956 (fax)

Loving Your Disabled Child (LYDC)
4715 Crenshaw Boulevard
Los Angeles CA 90043
213-299-2925
213-299-4373 (fax)
lydc@pacbell.net

Matrix, Parent Network and Resource Center
555 Northgate Dr Ste A
San Rafael CA 94903
415-499-3877
415-507-9457 (fax)
matrix@marin.k-12.ca.us.
http://marin.org/matrix/

Parents Helping Parents—San Francisco
594 Monterey Blvd
San Francisco CA 94127
415-841-8820
415-841-8824 (fax)

Parents Helping Parents—Santa Clara
The Family Resource Center
3041 Olcott St
Santa Clara CA 95054-3222
408-727-5775
408-727-7655 (TDD)
408-727-0182 (fax)
info@php.com
www.portal.com/~cbntmkr/php.html

Parents of Watts (POW)
10828 Lou Dillon Avenue
Los Angeles CA 90059
213-566-7556
213-566-4223
213-569-3982 (fax)

TASK
100 W Cerritos Ave
Anaheim CA 92805-6546
714-533-TASK (8275)
714-533-2533 (fax)
taskca@aol.com

TASK- San Diego
3750 Convoy St Ste 303
San Diego CA 92111
619-874-2386
619-874-2375 (fax)

Vietnamese Parents of Disabled Children (VPDC)
314 Gina Drive
Carson CA 90745-3617
310-533-1348
310-370-6704
310-542-0522 (fax)
lchu@earthlink.net

COLORADO

PEAK Parent Center, Inc.
6055 Lehman Drive Ste 101
Colorado Springs CO 80918
719-531-9400
719-531-9403 (TDD)
800-284-0251
719-531-9452 (fax)
PKPARENT@aol.com

CONNECTICUT

Connecticut Parent Advocacy Center, Inc. (CPAC)
5 Church Lane Ste 4
PO Box 579
East Lyme CT 06333
203-739-3089
800-445-2722 (CT only)
860-739-7460 (fax)
cpacinc@aol.com

DELAWARE

Parent Information Center (PIC) of Delaware, Inc.
700 Barksdale Road Ste 3
Newark DE 19711
302-366-0152
302-366-0178 (TDD)
302-366-0276 (fax)

DISTRICT OF COLUMBIA

COPE
300 I Street NE Ste 112
Washington DC 20002
202-543-6482
800-515-COPE (National)
202-543-6682 (fax)
cope@pop.erols.com

FLORIDA

COFFO, Inc.
305 South Flagler Avenue
PO Box 900368
Homestead FL 33090
305-246-0357
305-246-2445 (fax)

**Family Network on Disabilities of
Florida**
2735 Whitney Road
Clearwater FL 24620
813-523-1130
800-285-5736 (FL only)
813-523-8687 (fax)
FND@gate.net
http://www.naples.net/presents/
FamilyNetwork/index.html

Parent Empowerment Project
332 West Alvarez Avenue
Clewiston FL 33440
941-983-4417
fnd@gate.net

GEORGIA

**Parents Educating Parents (PEP)--
arc/georgia**
PO Box 43663
Atlanta GA 30336
404-761-3150
404-767-2258 (fax)

HAWAII

**AWARE/Learning Disabilities
Association of Hawaii**
200 N Vineyard Blvd Ste 310
Honolulu HI 96817
808-536-2280
808-537-6780 (fax)

IDAHO

Idaho Parents Unlimited, Inc. (IPUL)
Parents Education & Resource Center
4696 Overland Rd Ste 478
Boise ID 83705
208-342-5884
800-242-IPUL (4785)
208-342-1408 (fax)

ILLINOIS

Designs for Change
6 N Michigan Ave Ste 1600
Chicago IL 60602
312-857-9292
312-857-1013 (TDD)
312-857-9299 (fax)
DFC1@aol.com

**Family Resource Center on Disabilities
(FRCD)**
20 East Jackson Blvd Rm 900
Chicago IL 60604
312-939-3513
312-939-3519 (TDD/TTY)
312-939-7297 (fax)

Family T.I.E.S. Network
830 South Spring Street
Springfield IL 62704
800-865-7842
217-544-6018 (fax)
ftiesn@aol.com

**National Center for Latinos with
Disabilities**
1921 South Blue Island
Chicago IL 60608
312-666-3393
312-666-1788 (TDD)
312-666-1787 (fax)

INDIANA

IN*SOURCE
809 N Michigan St
South Bend IN 46601-1036
219-234-7101
800-332-4433 (IN only)
219-234-7279 (fax)
insource@inspeced.ccmail.
compuserve.com

IOWA

SEEK Parent Center
1011 W. 19th
Cedar Falls IA 50613
319-277-8362

KANSAS

Families Together, Inc.
501 Jackson Ste 400
Topeka KS 66603
913-233-4777
800-264-6343 (KS only)
913-233-4787 (fax)
family@smartnet.net

KENTUCKY

(KY-SPIN)
2210 Goldsmith Lane Ste 118
Louisville KY 40218
502-456-0923
800-525-7746
502-456-0893 (fax)

LOUISIANA

Project PROMPT
4323 Division Street Ste 110
Metairie LA 70124-3179
504-888-9111
800-766-7736
504-888-0246 (fax)
fhfgno@ix.netcom.com

Pyramid Parent Training Project
3132 Napolean Avenue
New Orleans LA 70125

504-895-5970
504-899-5739 (fax)
dmarkey404@aol.com

MAINE

**Special-Needs Parent Information
Network (SPIN)**
PO Box 2067
Augusta ME 04330-2067
207-582-2504
800-325-SPIN (TDD-ME only)
207-582-3638 (fax)
lachance@SATURN.caps.me.edu

MARYLAND

The Parents' Place of Maryland
7257 Parkway Dr Ste 210
Hanover MD 21076
410-712-0900
410-712-0902 (fax)
parplace@aol.com

MASSACHUSETTS

**Federation for Children with Special
Needs**
1135 Tremont St
Suite 420
Boston,MA 02120
617-236-7210
800-331-0688 (MA only)
617-592-2094 (fax)
ahiggins@fcsn.org
fcsninfo@fcsn.org
kidinfo@fcsn.org
http://www.fcsn.org

IPEST
Martha's Vineyard
108 Lake Street
PO Box 4081
Vineyard Haven MA 02586
508-696-6527
508-696-7437 (fax)
ckennedy@tiac.net

MICHIGAN

CAUSE
3303 W Saginaw St Ste F1
Lansing MI 48917-2303
517-485-4084
800-221-9105 (MI only)
517-886-9775 (fax)

Parents are Experts/Parents Training
 Parents Project
23077 Greenfield Rd Ste 205
Southfield MI 48075-3744
810-557-5070
810-557-4456 (fax)

UPBEATT
9950 Fielding
Detroit MI 48228-1214
313-835-6898
313-837-0358
313-837-1164 (Call first) (fax)
upbeatt@aol.com

MINNESOTA

PACER Center
4826 Chicago Avenue South
Minneapolis MN 55417-1098
612-827-2966
800-53-PACER (MN only)
612-827-3065 (fax)
mnpacer@edu.gte.netgoldb009@
gold.tc.umn.edu
http://freenet.msp.mn.us/ip/family/pacer/

MISSISSIPPI

Parent Partners
3111 N State Street
Jackson MS 39216
601-366-5707
601-362-7361 (fax)

Project Empower
1427 South Main Ste 8
Greenville MS 38702-0851
601-332-4852
800-337-4852
601-332-1622 (fax)

MISSOURI

Missouri Parents Act (MPACT)

MPACT—Springfield Office
2100 S Brentwood Ste G
Springfield MO 65804
417-882-7434
800-743-7634 (MO only)
417-882-8413 (fax)

MPACT—St Louis Office
8631 Delmar Ste 300
St Louis MO 63124
314-997-7622
314-997-5518 (fax)

Parent Education and Advocacy
 Resource Support Project (PEARS)

MPACT—Kansas City Office
3100 Main Ste 303
Kansas City MO 64111
816-531-7070
816-931-2992 (TDD)
800-995-3160 (MO only)
816-531-4777 (fax)

MONTANA

Parents Let's Unite for Kids (PLUK)
MSU-B/SPED Rm 183
1500 N 30th St
Billings MT 59101-0298
406-657-2055
800-222-7585 (MT only)
406-657-2061 (fax)
PLUKMT@aol.com

NEBRASKA

Nebraska Parents' Center
3610 Dodge Street
Omaha NE 68131
402-346-0525
800-284-8520
402-346-5253 (fax)

NEVADA

Nevada Parents Encouraging Parents (PEP)
6910 Edna Avenue
Las Vegas NV 89117
702-248-6711
702-367-9812 (fax)
eppie3@aol.com

NEW HAMPSHIRE

NH-Parent Information Center (PIC)
151 A Manchester Street
PO Box 2405
Concord NH 03302-2405
603-224-6299
800-232-0986 (NH only)
603 224-7005
603-224-4365 (fax)
picnh@aol.com

NEW JERSEY

Statewide Parent Advocacy Network, Inc. (SPAN)
35 Halsey Street 4th Flr
Newark NJ 07102
201-642-8100
800-654-SPAN (NJ only)
201-642-8080 (fax)

NEW MEXICO

EPICS
Southwest Communication Resources, Inc.
2000 Camino del Pueblo
PO Box 788
Bernalillo NM 87004
505-867-3396 ext 4
800-765-7320
505-867-3398 (fax)
s1c2r3@indirect.com

Parents Reaching Out Project ADOBE
1000A Main Street, NW
Campbell Hall Bldg 14 Ste A
Los Lunas NM 87031-7477
505-865-3700

800-524-5176 (NM only)
505-865-3737 (fax)
jroot@aol.com

NEW YORK

Advocates for Children of New York
105 Court St Rm 402
Brooklyn NY 11201
718-729-8866
718-729-8931 (fax)

Parent Network Center (PNC)
250 Delaware Ave Ste 3
Buffalo NY 14202-1515
716-853-1570
800-724-7408 (NY only)
716-853-1573 (TDD)
716-853-1574 (fax)
bk066@freenet.buffalo.edu

Resources for Children with Special Needs
200 Park Ave S Ste 816
New York NY 10003
212-677-4650
212-254-4070 (fax)

Sinergia
15 West 65th Street, 6th Floor
New York NY 10023
212-496-1300
212-496-5608 (fax)
sinergia@panix.com
http://www.panix.com/~sinergia

United We Stand
c/o Francis of Paola Preschool
201 Conselyea Street
Brooklyn NY 11211
718-782-1462
718-782-8044 (fax)
uwsofny@aol.com

NORTH CAROLINA

Exceptional Children's Assistance Center (ECAC)
121 Depot Street
PO Box 16
Davidson NC 28036

704-892-1321
800-962-6817 (NC only)
704-892-5028 (fax)
ECAC1@aol.com

NORTH DAKOTA

Pathfinder PTI
Pathfinder Family Center
Arrowhead Shopping Center
1600 2nd Avenue, SW
Minot ND 58701
701-852-9426
701-852-9436 (TDD)
701-838-9324 (fax)
kjel100w@wonder.em.cdc.gov

OHIO

Child Advocacy Center
1821 Summit Road Ste 303
Cincinnati OH 45237
513-821-2400
513-821-2442 (fax)
CADCenter@aol.com

**Ohio Coalition for the Education of
   Children with Disabilities (OCECD)**
Bank One Building
165 West Center St Ste 302
Marion OH 43302-3741
614-382-5452
800-374-2806
614-383-6421 (fax)

PUSH
2302 Osceola Ave.
Cleveland OH 44108
216-761-9041
216-761-2010 (fax)

OKLAHOMA

**Parents Reaching Out in Oklahoma
   Project (PRO-OK)**
1917 South Harvard Avenue
Oklahoma City OK 73128

405-681-9710
800-PL94-142
405-685-4006 (fax)
prook1@aol.com

OREGON

Oregon COPE Project
999 Locust Street, NE Box B
Salem OR 97303
503-373-7477
503-391-0429 (fax)
cope@ncn.com

PENNSYLVANIA

Mentor Parent Program
Main Street
PO Box 718
Seneca PA 16346
814-676-8615
814-677-4465 (fax)

Parent Education Network
333 E 7th Avenue
York PA 17404
717-845-9722
800-522-5827 (PA only)
800-441-5027 (Spanish PA)
717 848-3654 (fax)

**Parents Union for Public Schools in
   Philadelphia, Inc.**
311 S Juniper St Ste 602
Philadelphia PA 19107
215-546-1166
215-731-1688 (fax)
CDavis@aol.com

PUERTO RICO

APNI
Box 21301
San Juan PR 00928-1301
787-763-4665
787-765-0345
809-765-0345 (fax)

RHODE ISLAND

Rhode Island Parent Information Network (RIPIN)
500 Prospect Street
Pawtucket RI 02860
401-727-4144
401-727-4151 (TDD)
800-464-3399 (RI only)
401-727-4040 (fax)

SOUTH CAROLINA

PRO-Parents
2712 Middleburg Dr Ste 102
Columbia SC 29204
803 779-3859
800 759-4776 (SC only)
803 252-4513 (fax)
PROParents@aol.com

SOUTH DAKOTA

Tokata Ho/Voices of the Future Parent Training Project
PO Box 937
Pine Ridge SD 57770
605-867-1521 (Mon 3-6)
605-867-1314 (T-F 830-4)
605-867-5832 (fax)

South Dakota Parent Connection
3701 W 49th Ste 200B
Sioux Falls SD 57118-4813
605-361-3171
800-640-4553 (SD only)
605-361-2928 (fax)
jdiehl@sdparentconnection.com
http://www.dakota.net/sdpc

TENNESSEE

Support & Training for Exceptional Parents (STEP)
111 Village Drive Ste 5
Greeneville TN 37745
423-639-0125
800-280-STEP (TN only)
423-639-2464

423-636-8217 (fax)
TNSTEP2@aol.com
http://www.sounddata.com/pti/

TEXAS

PATH/Partners Resource Network, Inc.
1090 Longfellow Dr Ste B
Beaumont TX 77706-4889
409 898-4684
409-898-4816 (TDD)
800-866-4726
409-898-4869 (fax)
PRN@TENET.edu

Project PODER
1017 N Main Ave Ste 207
San Antonio TX 78212
210-222-2637
800-682-9747 (TX only)
210-222-2638 (fax)

UTAH

Utah Parent Center (UPC)
2290 E 4500 S Ste 110
Salt Lake City UT 84117
801-272-1051
800-468-1160 (UT only)
801-272-8907 (fax)
upc@inconnect.com

VERMONT

Vermont Parent Information Center/ VPIC
The Chace Mill
1 Mill Street Ste A7
Burlington VT 05401
802-658-5315
800-639-7170 (VT only)
802 658-5395 (fax)

VIRGIN ISLANDS

VI Find
7th Street Sugar Estate
PO Box 11670
St Thomas USVI 00801
809-774-1162

809-774-1642 (TTY)
809-774-7844 (fax)

VIRGINIA

Parent Educational Advocacy Training Center (PEATC)
10340 Democracy Ln Ste 206Fairfax VA 22030
703-691-7826
800-869-6782 (VA only)
703-691-8148 (fax)
karp102w@wonder.em.cdc.gov
PEATCinc@aol.com

WASHINGTON

STOMP: Specialized Training of Military Parents
10209 Bridgeport Way SW Ste A5
Lakewood WA 98499-2327
206-588-1741
800-298-3543
206 984-7520 (fax)
Pavestomp@aol.com
http://www.nwrain.net/~wapave/index.html

Washington PAVE
6316 South 12th Street
Tacoma WA 98465
206-565-2266
800-5-PARENT (WA only)
206 566-8052 (fax)
wapave@nwrain.net
stomp@nwrain.net
http://www.nwrain.net/~wapave/index.html

WEST VIRGINIA

West Virginia Parent Training and Information (WVPTI)
371 Broaddus Ave
Clarksburg WV 26301
304-624-1436
304 624-1438 (fax)

WISCONSIN

Parent Education Project of Wisconsin (PEP-WI)
2192 S 60th St
West Allis WI 53219-1568
414-328-5520
800-231-8382
414-328-5527
414-328-5520 (fax)
patrice.colletti@enan.unm.edu
colletti@omnifest.uwm.edu

WYOMING

Wyoming Parent Information Center (PIC)
5 North Lobban
Buffalo WY 82834
307-684-2277
800-660-WPIC (WY only)
307 684-5314 (fax)
t.dawson@wyoming.com

Alliance for Technology Access Resource Centers

NATIONAL OFFICE:
2175 E Francisco Blvd Ste L
San Rafael CA 94901
415-455-4575
415-455-0491 (TTY)
atainfo@ataccess.org
http://www.ataccess.org

ALABAMA

Birmingham Alliance for Technology Access Center
Birmingham Independent Living Center
206 13th Street South
Birmingham AL 35233-1317
205-251-2223
dkessle1@ix.netcom.com

Technology Assistance for Special
Consumers
PO Box 443
Huntsville AL 35804
205-532-5996
tasc@traveller.com

ALASKA

Alaska Services for Enabling
Technology
PO Box 6485
Sitka AK 99835
907-747-7615
asetseak@aol.com

ARIZONA

Technology Access Center of Tucson
PO Box 13178
4710 East 29th Street
Tucson AZ 85732-3178
520-745-5588 ext. 412
tactaz@aol.com

ARKANSAS

Technology Resource Center
c/o Arkansas Easter Seal Society
3920 Woodland Heights Road
Little Rock AR 72212-2495
501-227-3600
atrce@aol.com

CALIFORNIA

Center for Accessible Technology
2547 8th St, 12-A
Berkeley CA 94710-2572
510-841-3224
cforat@aol.com
http://www.el.net/CAT

Computer Access Center
PO Box 5336
Santa Monica CA 90409
310-338-1597
cac@cac.org
http://www.cac.org

Sacramento Center for Assistive
Technology
701 Howe Avenue Ste E-5
Sacramento CA 95825
916-927-7228
scat@quiknet.com
http://www.sanjuan.edu/scat/index.html

SACC * Assistive Technology Center
Simi Valley Hospital North Campus
PO Box 1325
Simi Valley CA 93062
805-582-1881
dssaccca@aol.com

Special Technology Center
590 Castro Street
Mountain View CA 94041
415-961-6789
stcca@aol.com

Team of Advocates for Special Kids
100 W Cerritos Ave
Anaheim CA 92805-6546
714-533-8275
taskca@aol.com

FLORIDA

CITE, Inc.—Center for Independence,
Technology & Education
215 E New Hampshire St
Orlando FL 32804
407-898-2483
comcite@aol.com

GEORGIA

Tech-Able, Inc.
1140 Ellington Dr.
Conyers GA 30207
770-922-6768
techable@onramp.net
http://www.onramp.net/tech-able

HAWAII

Aloha Special Technology Access
Center
710 Green St.

Honolulu HI 96813
808-523-5547
stachi@aol.com
http://www.aloha.net/~stachi

IDAHO

United Cerebral Palsy of Idaho, Inc.
5530 West Emerald
Boise ID 83706
ucpidaho@aol.com

ILLINOIS

Northern Illinois Center for Adaptive Technology
3615 Louisiana Road
Rockford IL 61108-6195
815-229-2163
ilcat@aol.com

Technical Aids & Assistance for the Disabled Center
1950 West Roosevelt Road
Chicago IL 60608
312-421-3373
800-346-2939
taad@interaccess.com
http://homepage.interaccess.com/users/~taad

INDIANA

Assistive Technology Training and Information Center
Attic: A Resource Center on Independent Living
PO Box 2441
Vincennes IN 47591
812-886-0575
inattic1@aol.com

KANSAS

Technology Resource Solutions for People
1710 West Schilling Road
Salina KS 67401
913-827-9383
trspks@aol.com

KENTUCKY

Bluegrass Technology Center
169 N Limestone Street
Lexington KY 40507
606-255-9951
bluegrass@uky.campus.mci.net
http://www.kde.state.ky.us/assistive/Assistive_Technology.html

Enabling Technologies of Kentuckiana
Louisville Free Public Library
301 York Street
Louisville KY 40203-2257
502-574-1637
800-890-1840 (KY only)
502-582-2448
entech@iglou.com
http://www.kde.state.ky.us/assistive/Assistive_Technology.html

SpeciaLink
36 W 5th Street
Covington KY 41011
606-491-2464
speclink@one.net
WWW: http://www.kde.state.ky.us/assistive/Assistive_Technology.html

Western Kentucky Assistive Technology Consortium
PO Box 266
Murray KY 42071
502-759-4233
wkatc@mursuky.campus.mci.net
http://www.kde.state.ky.us/assistive/Assistive_Technology.html

MARYLAND

Learning Independence Through Computers, Inc. (LINC)
28 E Ostend St Ste 140
Baltimore MD 21230
410-659-5462
410-659-5469 (TTY)
lincmd@aol.com
http://www.linc.org

MASSACHUSETTS

Massachusetts Special Technology Access Center
12 Mudge Way 1–6
Bedford MA 01730-2138
617-275-2446
mastac@ma.ultranet.com
http://www.ultranet.com/~mastac/

MICHIGAN

Living & Learning Resource Centre
PIAM
1023 S US 27
St Johns MI 48879-2424
517-224-0333
800-833-1996(MI only)
llrcmi@aol.com

MINNESOTA

PACER Computer Resource Center
4826 Chicago Avenue South
Minneapolis MN 55417-1055
612-827-2966
pacercrc@aol.com
http://www.pacer.org/crc/crc.htm

MISSOURI

Technology AccessCenter
12110 Clayton Road
St Louis MO 63131-2599
314-569-8404
314-569-8446 (TTY)
mostltac@aol.com

MONTANA

Parents, Let's Unite for Kids
MSU-B/SPED Rm 183
1500 N 30th St
Billings MT 59101-0298
406-657-2055
800-222-7585 (MT only)
406-657-2061 (fax)
plukmt@aol.com

NEW JERSEY

Computer Center for People With Disabilities
c/o Family Resource Associates, Inc.
35 Haddon Avenue
Shrewsbury NJ 07702-4007
908-747-5310
ccdanj@aol.com

Center for Enabling Technology
622 Route 10 West Ste 22B
Whippany NJ 07981
201-428-1455
201-428-1450 (TTY)
cetnj@aol.com

NEW YORK

Techspress Resource Ctr for Independent Living
409 Columbia Street
PO Box 210
Utica NY 13503-0210
315-797-4642
txprsny@aol.com

NORTH CAROLINA

Carolina Computer Access Center
Metro School
700 East Second Street
Charlotte NC 28202-2826
704-342-3004
ccacnc@aol.com
http://www.charweb.org/health/
  healthindex.html

OHIO

Technology Resource Center
301 Valley St
Dayton OH 45404-1840
513-222-5222
trcdoh@aol.com

RHODE ISLAND

TechACCESS Center of Rhode Island
300 Richmond St

Providence RI 02903-4222
401-273-1990
800-916-TECH (RI only)
accessri@aol.com
techaccess@ids.net

TENNESSEE

East Tennessee Technology Access
    Center, Inc.
3525 Emory Road NW
Powell TN 37849
423-947-2191
etstactn@aol.com
http://www.korrnet.org/ettac/

Technology Access Center of Middle
    Tennessee
Fountain Square Ste 126
2222 Metrocenter Blvd
Nashville TN 37228
615-248-6733
800-368-4651
tactn@aol.com

West Tennessee Special Technology
    Access Resource Center (STAR)
PO Box 3683
60 Lynoak Cove
Jackson TN 38305
901-668-3888
800-464-5619
startn@usit.net
http://erc.jscc.cc.tn.us/jfn/star/

UTAH

The Computer Center for Citizens
    with Disabilities
c/o Utah Center for Assistive Technology
2056 South 1100 East
Salt Lake City UT 84106
801-485-9152
cboogaar@usoe.k12.ut.us

VIRGIN ISLANDS

Virgin Islands Resource Center for the
    Disabled, Inc.
PO Box 1825
St Thomas VI 00803
809-777-2253

VIRGINIA

Tidewater Center for Technology
    Access
Special Education Annex
960 Windsor Oaks Blvd
Virginia Beach VA 23462
757-474-8650
tcta@aol.com

WEST VIRGINIA

Eastern Panhandle Technology Access
    Center, Inc.
PO Box 987
300 S Lawrence St
Charles Town WV 25414
304-725-6473
eptac@earthlink.net

State Tech Act Projects

ALABAMA

Statewide Technology Access and
    Response
2125 E South Blvd
PO Box 20752
Montgomery AL 36120-0752
334-613-3480
334-613-3485
alstar@mont.mindspring.com
http://www.mindspring.com/~alstar

ALASKA

Assistive Technologies of Alaska
2217 E Tudor Rd Ste 5
Anchorage AK 99507
907-563-0138

907-563-0699 (fax)
ata@dvr@corcom.net
http://www.corcom.net

AMERICAN SAMOA

American Samoa Assistive Technology
  Projects
Dept of Human Resources
PO Box 4561
Pago Pago 96799
American Samoa
011-684-699-1376
011-684-699-1376(fax)
voc.rehab@601.com

ARIZONA

Arizona Technology Access Program
2600 N Wyatt Dr
Tucson AZ 85712
520-324-3170
520-324-3177 (TTY)
520-324-3176 (fax)
demetras@ccit.arizona.edu
http://www.nau.edu/~ihd/aztap.html

ARKANSAS

Increasing Capabilities Access Network
2201 Brookwood Dr Ste 117
Little Rock AR 72202
501-666-8868
501-666-5319 (fax)

CALIFORNIA

California Assistive Technology System
PO Box 944222
Sacramento CA 94244-2220
916-324-3062
916-323-0914 (fax)
doroa.dorcats@hw1.cahwnet.gov

COLORADO

Colorado Assistive Technology Project
1391 N Spear Blvd 350
Denver CO 80204
303-534-1027

303-534-1063 (TTY)
800-255-3477 (CO Only)
303-534-1075 (fax)
rmrti@essex.uchsc.edu

CONNECTICUT

Tech Act Project
10 Griffin Rd N
Windsor CT 06095
860-298-2042
800-537-2549
860-298-9590 (fax)
jficarro@aol.com
http://www.ucc.uconn.edu/~wwwpcse/
  techact.html

DELAWARE

Delaware Assistive Technology
  Initiative
1600 Rockland Rd
PO Box 269
Wilmington DE 19899-0269
302-651-6790
302-651-6794 (TDD)
800-870-DATI (DE only)
302-651-6793 (fax)
dati@asel.udel.edu/dati/

DISTRICT OF COLUMBIA

Partnership for Assistive Technology
801 Pennsylvania Ave SE
Ste 300
Washington DC 20003
202-546-9163
202-546-9169 (fax)
alexlugo@dcpat.org
http://www.cdd.sc.edu

FLORIDA

Florida Alliance for Assistive Services
  and Technology (FAAST) Program
2002 Old St Augustine Rd Bldg A
Tallahassee FL 32399-0696
904-487-3278
904-488-8380 (TDD)

904-921-7214 (fax)
FAAST@freenet.scri.fsu.edu
http://pegasus.cc.ucf.edu/~faasstcat/
fcenters/thome.html

GEORGIA

Tools for Life
2 Peachtree St NE Ste 23-411
Atlanta GA 30303
404-657-3084
404-657-3086 (fax)
102476.1737@compuserve.com
http://www.gatfl.org

HAWAII

**Assistive Technology Training and
Services (HATTS) Project**
677 Ala Moana Blvd Ste 403
Honolulu HI 96813
808-532-7110
808-645-3007 (neighbor Islands)
808-532-7120 (fax)
bfl@pixi.com

IDAHO

Idaho Assistive Technology Project
129 W Third St
Moscow ID 83843
208-885-3573
800-432-6324
208-885-3628 (fax)
seile861@uidaho.edu
http://www.ets.uidaho.edu/icdd/

ILLINOIS

Illinois Assistive Technology Project
528 S Fifth St Ste 100
Springfield IL 62701
217-522-7985
217-522-9966 (TTY)
800-852-5110 (IL only)
217-522-8067 (fax)
iatp@midwest.net

INDIANA

**ATTAIN: Accessing Technology
Through Awareness in Indiana
Project**
1815 N Meridian St Ste 200
Indianapolis IN 46202
317-921-9766
800-747-3333 (TDD only)
800-528-8246 (IN only)
317-921-8774 (fax)
cfulford@vunet.vinu.edu

IOWA

Iowa Program for Assistive Technology
University Hospital School
Iowa City IA 52242-1011
319-356-4382
800-348-7193
319-356-8284 (fax)

KANSAS

Assistive Technology for Kansas
2601 Gabriel
Parsons KS 67357
316-421-8367
316-421-0954 (fax)
ssimons@parsons.lsi.ukansd.edu
http://www.lsi.ukans.edu/lsi/athp/htm

KENTUCKY

**Kentucky Technology Services
Network (KATS)**
8412 Westfort Rd
Louisville KY 40242
502-327-0022
502-327-9991 (fax)

LOUISIANA

**LATAN: Louisiana Assistive
Technology Access Network**
3042 Old Forge Rd Ste B
PO Box 14115
Baton Rouge LA 70898-4115
504-925-9500
800-270-6185

504-925-9560 (fax)
latanstate@aol.com

MAINE

**Consumer Information and
Technology Training Exchange**
46 University Dr
Augusta ME 04330
207-621-3195
207-621-3193 (fax)

MARYLAND

**Maryland Technology Assistance
Program**
300 W Lexington St Box 10
Baltimore MD 21201
410-333-4975
800-TECH-TAP
410-333-6674 (fax)
mdtap@clark.net
http://www.mdtap.org

MASSACHUSETTS

**Massachusetts Assistive Technology
Partnership (MATP)**
1295 Boylston St Ste 310
Boston MA 02215
617-355-7820
617-355-7301 (TTY)
617-355-6345 (fax)
brewer_ju@a1.tch.harvard.edu

MICHIGAN

Rehabilitation Services
PO Box 30010
Lansing MI 48909
517-373-2414
800-605-6722 (TTY)
800-562-7860 (MI Upper Peninsula)
517-373-0565 (fax)
http://www.mrs.mjc.state.mi.us

MINNESOTA

Minnesota Star Program
300 Centennial Bldg 3rd Fl

658 Cedar St
St Paul MN 55155
612-296-2771
612-296-9962 (TDD)
612-296-9478 (TTY)
800-657-3862 (MN only)
800-657-3895 (TTY MN only)
612-282-6671 (fax)
mnstars@edu.gte.net
http://www.state.mn.us/ebranch/admin/
assitivetechnology.html

MISSISSIPPI

Project Start
PO Box 1698
Jackson MS 39215-1698
601-853-5171
601-853-5158 (fax)

MISSOURI

Missouri Assistive Technology Project
4731 S Cochise Ste 114
Independence MO 64055
816-373-5193
816-373-9315 (TTY)
816-373-9314 (fax)
matpmo@qni.com

MONTANA

**MonTECH: Technology Related
Assistance Program for Persons with
Disabilities**
University of Montana
634 Eddy Ave
Missoula MT 59812
406-243-5676
800-732-0323
800-961-9610 (BBS)
montech@selway.umt.edu

NEBRASKA

Nebraska Assistive Technology Project
301 Centennial Mall S
PO Box 94987
Lincoln NE 65809-4987

402-471-0734
800-742-7594 (NE only)
402-471-0117 (fax)
atp@nde4.nde.state.ne.us
http://www.nde.state.ne.us/ATP/
  TACHome.html

NEVADA

Nevada Assistive Technology Project
711 S Stewart
Carson City NV 89710
702-687-4452
702-687-3262 (fax)

NEW HAMPSHIRE

Alliance for Assistive Technology
10 Ferry St Ste 321 Unit #25
Concord NH 03301-5081
603-228-2088
800-427-3338
603-228-2468 (fax)
Imarko@nhaat.mv.com

NEW JERSEY

Technology Assistive Resource Program
CN 398
Trenton NJ 08625
609-292-4967
609-292-2919 (TTY)
609-292-8347 (fax)
lav42prg@concentric.net
http:www.wnjpin.state.nj.us

NEW MEXICO

New Mexico Technology Assistance
  Program
435 St Michael's Dr Bldg D
Santa Fe NM 87505
505-827-3532
800-866-2253
800-659-4915 (TDD)
505-827-3746 (fax)
nmdvrtap@aol.com

NEW YORK

New York State Office of Advocate for
  Persons with Disabilities
One Empire State Plaza
Ste 1001
Albany NY 12223-1150
518-474-2825
518-473-4231 (TTY)
800-522-4369 (NY only)
518-473-6005 (fax)
d.buck@oapwd.state.ny.us

NORTH CAROLINA

North Carolina Assistive Technology
  Project
1110 Navaho Dr Ste 101
Raleigh NC 27609-7322
919-850-2787
919-850-2792 (fax)
http://www2.coastalnet.com/~cn3106

NORTH DAKOTA

Interagency Project for Assistive
  Technology
PO Box 743
Cavalier ND 58220
701-265-4807
800-265-4728
701-265-3150 (fax)
lee@pioneer.state.nd.us

OHIO

TRAIN: Technology Related
  Assistance Information Network
1224 Kinnear Rd
Columbus OH 43212
614-292-2426
614-292-3162 (TTY)
800-784-3425
614-292-5866 (fax)
dmkahl@mailcar.ovl.osc.edu
http://pages.prodigy.com/ability

OKLAHOMA

Oklahoma ABLE Tech
OK State University
1514 W Hall of Fame
Stillwater OK 74078-0618
405-744-9355
800-257-1705
405-744-7670 (fax)
rogers@okway.okstate.edu

OREGON

Access Technologies Inc. TALN Project
1257 Ferry St SE
Salem OR 97310
503-361-1201
800-677-7512 (OR only)
ati@orednet.org

PENNSYLVANIA

**Pennsylvania Initiative on Assistive
Technology**
Ritter Annex Room 423
Temple University
Philadelphia PA 19122
800-204-PIAT
800-750-PIAT (TTY)
215-204-9371 (fax)
piat@astro.ocis.temple.edu

PUERTO RICO

**Puerto Rico Assistive Technology
Project**
University of Puerto Rico
PO Box 365067
San Juan PR 00963-5067
787-764-6035
787-754-8034 (TTY)
787-754-8035 (fax)
PRATP@rcmad.upr.clu.edu

RHODE ISLAND

**Assistive Technology Access
Partnership**
40 Fountain St
Providence RI 02903-1898

401-421-7005
401-421-7016 (TTY)
401-421-9259 (fax)
jfarrell@ors.state.ri.us

SOUTH CAROLINA

**South Carolina Assistive Technology
Project**
Center for Developmental Disabilities
Columbia SC 29208
803-935-5231
803-935-5342 (fax)
scatp@scsn.net

SOUTH DAKOTA

DakotaLink
1825 Plaza Blvd
Rapid City SD 57702
605-394-1876
800-645-0673 (SD only)
605-394-5315 (fax)
jjohnson@sdtie.sdserv.org
http://www.tie.net/dakotalink

TENNESSEE

Technology Access Project
Andrew Johnson Tower 11th Fl 710
James Robertson Pkwy
Nashville TN 37243-0675
615-532-6555
615-741-4566 (TDD)
800-732-5059
akoshakj@mail.state.tn.us

TEXAS

Texas Assistive Technology Partnership
SZB 252 D5100
Austin TX 78712-1290
512-471-7621
512-471-1844 (TDD)
800-828-7839
512-471-7549 (fax)
johnz@utxvms.cc.utexas.ed
http://www.edbutexas.edu/coe/depts/
sped/tatp/tatp.html

UTAH

Utah Assistive Technology Program
Utah State University
Logan UT 84322-6855
801-797-3824
801-797-2355 (fax)
mmenlove@cc.usu.edu

VERMONT

Vermont Assistive Technology Project
103 S Main St
Waterbury VT 05671-2305
802-241-2620
802-241-2174 (fax)
lynnec@dad.state.vt.us

VIRGINIA

Assistive Technology System
8004 Franklin Farms Dr
PO Box K-300
Richmond VA 23288-0300
804-662-9990
800-435-8490
804-662-9478 (fax)

WASHINGTON

**Washington Assistive Technology
Alliance**
PO Box 45340
Olympia WA 98504-5340
360-438-8000
800-841-8345 (WA only)
360-438-8007 (fax)
nacewl@fcs.dshs.wa.gov

WEST VIRGINIA

**West Virginia Assistive Technology
System (WVATS)**
Airport Research and Office Park 955
Hartman Run Rd
Morgantown WV 26505
304-293-4692
304-293-7294 (fax)
stewiat@wvnvm.wvnet.edu

WISCONSIN

WisTech
PO Box 7852
Madison WI 45707-7852
608-243-5676
608-243-5680 (fax)
trampf@aol.com

WYOMING

Wyoming New Options in Technology
1100 Herschler Bldg
Cheyenne WY 82002
307-777-6947
307-777-7155 (fax)
kmckin@missc.state.wy.us

Software/Hardware Vendors

The following is an abbreviated list of technology manufacturers and software publishers. For a more complete list we recommend you obtain the *Closing The Gap* Annual Resource Directory for $14.95. They produce a bi-monthly publication on microcomputer technology for people with special needs for $29/year. They may be contacted at:

Closing the Gap
PO Box 68
Henderson MN 56044
507-248-3294
507-248-3810 (fax)
info@closingthegap.com
http://www.closingthegap.com

Able Net, Inc.
1081 Tenth Avenue SE
Minneapolis MN 55414-1312
612-379-0956
800-322-0956
612-379-9143 (fax)
Augmentative Communication Switches

Toys
Environmental Control

ADAMLAB
33500 Van Born Road
PO Box 807
Wayne MI 48184
313-467-1415
313-326-2610 (fax)
Kaminsk@wcresa.K12.mk.us
http://www.cresa.K12.mi.us/adamlab
Augmentative Communication

American Printing House for the Blind
1839 Frankfort Ave
PO Box 6085
Louisville KY 40206-0085
502-895-2405
800-223-1839 (service)
800-572-0844 (sales)
502-899-2274 (fax)
info@aph.org
http://www.aph.org
Notetakers
Screen Readers
Speech Synthesizers
Talking Software

DU-IT Control Systems
8765 Twp Rd 513
Shreve OH 44676-9421
216-567-2001
216-567-9217 (fax)
Wheelchair controls
Switches
Environmental Controls

Arkenstone, Inc.
555 Oakmead Pkwy
Sunnyvale CA 94086-4023
408-245-5900
800-444-4443
800-833-2753 (TDD)
408-328-8484 (fax)
info@arkenstone.org
http://www.arkenstone.org
Reading Machines

Arctic Technologies
55 Park Street
Troy MI 48083
810-588-7370
810-588-2650 (fax)
Screen Enlargement programs
Screen Readers
Speech Synthesizers

Articulate Systems, Inc.
600 West Cummings Park, Ste 4500
Woburn, MA 01801
800-443-7077
617-935-5656
617-935-0490 (fax)
Voice Recognition

Blazie Engineering, Inc.
105 E Jarrettsville Road
Forrest Hill MD 21050
410-893-9333
410-836-5040 (fax)
info@Blazie.com
http://www.blazie.com
Notetakers
Braille Embossers, Translators
Screen Readers

Broderbund Software, Inc.
500 Redwood Blvd.
PO Box 6121
Novato CA 94948-6121
415-382-4400
800-521-6263
415-382-4582 (fax)
Educational Software

Colorado Easter Seal Society, Inc.
Center for Adapted Technology
5755 W Alameda
Lakewood CO 80226
303-233-1666
303-233-1028 (fax)
catlab@cess.org
http://www2.coeastseal.org/orgs/cess/
Public Domain Software

Davidson & Associates, Inc.
19840 Pioneer Avenue
Torrance CA 90503
310-793-0600
800-545-7677
310-793-0603 (fax)
pr@davd.com
http://www.davd.com
Reading Comprehension Programs
Talking and Large Print Word Processors
Writing Composition Programs

Don Johnston, Inc.
1000 N Rand Road Bldg 115
PO Box 639
Wauconda IL 60084
847-526-2682
800-999-4660
847-526-4177 (fax)
DJDE@aol.com
http://www.donjohnston.com
Keyboard Additions
Alternate Keyboards
Reading Comprehension Programs
Switches, Switch Software
Interface Devices
Talking and Large Print Word Processors
Word Prediction Programs
Writing Composition Programs

Dragon Systems
320 Nevada Street
Newton, MA 02160
617-965-5200
617-630-9707 (fax)
info@dragonsys.com
http://www.dragonsys.com
Voice Recognition

Edmark Corporation
PO Box 97021
Redmond WA 98073-9721
206-556-8427
206-556-8402 (TT)
800-426-0856
206-556-8430 (fax)

maryannt@edmark.com
http://www.edmark.com
Menu Management Programs
Reading Comprehension programs
Touch Screens
Switches, Switch Software
Educational Software

Educational Resources
PO Box 1900
Elgin IL 60121-1900
800-624-2926
847-888-8499 (fax)
http://wwwedresources.com
Educational Software/Hardware
Special Needs Software/Hardware

Franklin Learning Resources
One Franklin Plaza
Burlington NJ 08016-4907
800-266-5626
609-239-5943 (fax)
Talking Dictionaries
Electronic Reference Tools

Gus Communications
1006 Lonetree Ct
Bellingham WA 98226
360-715-8580
360-715-9633 (fax)
gus@gusinc.com
http://www.gusinc.com
Interface Devices
Augmentative Communication Software
Speech and Access Utilities

GW Micro
725 Airport North Office Park
Fort Wayne IN 46825
219-489-3671
219-489-2608 (fax)
support@gwmicro.com
http://www.gwmicro.com
Screen Readers
Speech Synthesizers
Braille Embossers, Translators

Hartley
9920 Pacific Heights Blvd
San Diego CA 92121-4330
619-587-0087
800-247-1380
619-622-7873 (fax)
Reading Comprehension Programs
Talking and Large Print Word Processors

Henter-Joyce, Inc.
11800 31st Court N
St Petersburg FL 33702
813-572-8900
800-336-5658
813-528-8901 (fax)
info@hj.com
http://www.hj.com
Screen Readers

Humanities Software
PO Box 950
Hood River OR 97031
541-386-6737
800-245-6737
541-386-1410 (fax)
info@humanitiessoftware.com
Writing Composition/Reading Programs

HumanWare, Inc.
6245 King Road
Loomis CA 95650
916-652-7253
800-722-3393
916-652-7296 (fax)
http://www.humanware.com
CCTVs
Screen Readers
Speech Synthesizers
Notetakers
Refreshable Braille Displays
Braille Embossers, Translators
Screen Enlargement Programs

IBM Special Needs Systems
11400 Burnet Rd Bldg 904
Austin TX 78758
800-426-4832
800-426-4833 (TDD)

Access Utilities
Keyguards
Screen Readers
Voice Recognition
Speech Therapy Software

IntelliTools
55 Leveroni Ct Ste 9
Novato CA 94949
415-382-5959
800-899-6687
415-382-5950 (fax)
info@intellitools.com
http://www.intellitools.com
Alternate Keyboards
Keyboard Additions
Switches and Switch Software
Talking and Large Print Word Processors
Curriculum Access

Judy Lynn Software
PO Box 373
East Brunswick NJ 08816
908-390-8845
908-390-8845 (fax)
judylynn@castle.net
http://www.castle.net/~judylynn
Switch Software

Kurzweil Applied Intelligence
411 Waverley Oaks Road
Ste 330
Waltham MA 02154
617-893-5151
617-893-6525 (fax)
erikak@kurzweil.com
http://www.kurzweil.com
Voice Recognition
Reading Machine

LC Technologies/Eyegaze Systems
9455 Silver King Ct
Fairfax VA 22031
703-385-7133
800-733-5284
703-385-7137 (fax)
info@lcinc.com
http://www.lcinc.com
Eyegaze Computer System

LS&S Group
PO Box 673
Northbrook IL 60065
847-498-9777
800-468-4789
800-317-8533 (TTY)
847-498-1482 (fax)
lssgrp@aol.com
http://www.lssgroup.com
CCTVs
Screen Readers
Speech Synthesizers
Products for Hearing Impaired
Products for Visually Impaired

Laureate Learning Systems, Inc.
110 East Spring Street
Winooski VT 05404
802-655-4755
800-562-6801
802-655-4757 (fax)
Laureate@LLSys.com
http://www.LLSys.com
Reading Comprehension Programs
Switches, Switch Software
Talking Software

Learning Company
6493 Kaiser Drive
Fremont CA 94555
510-713-6011
800-227-5609
510-792-9628 (fax)
spena@learningco.com
http://www.learningco.com
Math Software
Reading Comprehension Programs
Writing Composition Programs

Learning Company School
6160 Summit Dr N
St Paul MN 55430-4003
612-569-1500
800-685-6322
612-569-1551 (fax)
pkallio@learningco.com
http://www.learningco.com
Educational Software

Madenta Communications
9411A-20th Avenue
Edmonton AB T6N 1E5 Canada
403-450-8926
800-661-8406
403-988-6182 (fax)
madenta@madenta.com
Environmental Controls
On-screen Keyboards
Pointing Devices

Mayer-Johnson Co.
PO Box 1579
Solana Beach CA 92075-1579
619-550-0084
619-550-0449 (fax)
mayerJ@aol.com
Augmentative Communication Tools

Microsystems Software, Inc.
600 Worcester Road
Framingham MA 01701
508-879-9000
800-828-2600
508-879-1069 (fax)
hware@microsys.com
http://www.handiware.com
Access Utilities
On-screen Keyboards
Screen Enlargement programs
Switches, Switch Software
Word Prediction Programs

Micro Talk
721 Olive
Texarkana TX 75501
903-792-2570
903-792-5140 (fax)
larry@screenaccess.com
http://www.screenaccess.com
Screen Readers

Optimum Resources Inc.
5 Hilltech Lane
Hilton Head Island SC 29926
803-689-8000
888-784-2592
803-689-8008 (fax)

stickyb@stickybear.com
http://www.stickybear.com
Educational Software

Prentke Romich Company
1022 Heyl Road
Wooster OH 44691
330-262-1984
800-262-1984
330-263-4829 (fax)
kgerrior@aol.com
Augmentative Communication
Environmental Controls
Joysticks
Keyboard Additions
Alternate Keyboards
Electronic Pointing Devices
Switches, Switch Software
Word Prediction Programs

R.J. Cooper and Associates
24843 Del Prado Ste 283
Dana Point CA 92629
714-240-4853
800-RJCOOPER
714-240-9785 (fax)
rj@rjcooper.com
http://www.rjcooper.com
Switches, Switch Software
Interface Devices
Alternative Keyboard

Roger Wagner Publishing, Inc.
1050 Pioneer Way Ste P
El Cajon CA 92020
800-421-6526
619-442-0525 (fax)
rwagnerinc@aol.com
Authoring Software

Sentient Systems Technology, Inc.
2100 Wharton Street Ste 630
Pittsburgh PA 15203
412-381-4883
412-381-5241 (fax)
sstsales@sentient-sys.com
http://www.sentient-sys.com
Augmentative Communication

Sunburst Communications
101 Castleton Street
Pleasantville NY 10570
914-747-3310
800-321-78511
sunburst4@aol.com
http://www.nysunburst.com
Educational Software

TASH International, Inc.
Unit 1, 91 Station Street
Ajax ON L1S 3H2 Canada
905-686-4129
800-463-5685
905-686-6895 (fax)
tashcan@aol.com
Environmental Controls
Joysticks
Keyboard Additions
Interface Devices
Switches, Switch Software
Augmentative Communication

TeleSensory
455 N Bernardo Avenue
Mountain View CA 94039
415-960-0920
415-969-9064 (fax)
sclark@telesensory.com
http://www.telesensory.com
Braille Embossers, Translators
CCTVs
Notetakers
Reading Machines
Refreshable Braille Displays
Screen Enlargement Programs
Screen Readers
Speech Synthesizers

Trace Research and Development Center
Room S-151 Waisman Center
1500 Highland Avenue
University of Wisconsin
Madison WI 53705-2280
608-262-6966
608-263-5408 (TDD)

608-262-8848 (fax)
info@trace.wisc.edu
http://trace.wisc.edu./
Information Resources

**UCLA Intervention Program for
Children with Disabilities**
1000 Veteran Avenue
Room 23-10
Los Angeles CA 90095
310-825-4821
310-206-7744 (fax)
twebb@pediatrics.medsscho.
ucla.edu
*Early Childhood Software
Switch Software*

Universal Learning Technology
39 Cross Street
Peabody MA 01960
508-538-0036
508-538-3110 (TTY)
508-531-0192 (fax)
ULT@cast.org
Software Text Reader

WesTest Engineering Corporation
810 W Shepard Ln
Farmington UT 84025
801-451-9191
801-451-9393
mary@darci.org
http://www.darci.org
Interface Devices

Words+, Inc.
40015 Sierra Highway B-45
Palmdale CA 93550-2117
800-869-8521
805-266-8969 (fax)
*Access Utilities
Alternate Keyboards
Interface Devices
Environmental Controls
Switches, Switch Software
Word Prediction Programs
Electronic Pointing Devices
Augmentative Communication*

Xerox Imaging Systems, Inc.
9 Centennial Drive
Peabody MA 01960
508-977-2000
800-343-0311
800-421-7323
508-977-2437 (fax)
hall@xis.xerox.com
http://www.xerox.com/products/other/
htm
Reading Machines

Zygo Industries, Inc.
PO Box 1008
Portland OR 97207
503-684-6006
800-234-6011
503-684-6011 (fax)
*Augmentative Communication
Environmental Controls
Alternate Keyboards
Switches, Switch Software*

Other Resources

**DB-LINK National Information
Clearinghouse on Children Who Are
Deaf-Blind**
Teaching Research
345 N Monmouth Ave
Monmouth OR 97361
800-438-9376
800-854-7013 (TTY)
503-838-8150 (fax)
leslieg@fsa.wosc.osshe.edu
Deaf-Blind Resources

LD Resources
Richard Wanderman
202 Lake Rd
New Preston CT 06777
860-868-3214
richard@ldresources.com
http://www.ldresources.com
Resources on Learning Disabilities

**National Library Service for the Blind
and Physically Handicapped**
The Library of Congress
1291 Taylor St NW
Washington DC 20542
202-707-5100
202-707-0712 (fax)
nls@loc.gov
Recorded Books and Magazines
Braille Books

**National Center to Improve Practise
(NCIP)**
Education Development Center
55 Chapel St
Newton MA 02158-1060
617-969-7100 ext 2387
617-969-4529 (TTY)
617-969-3440 (fax)
ncip@edc.org
http://www.edc.org/FSC/NCIP
Internet Resources

**Recording for the Blind & Dyslexic
(RFB&D)**
20 Roszel Rd
Princeton NJ 08540
609-452-0606
800-221-4792
609-520-7990 (fax)
custserv@rsbt.org
http://www.rfbd.org
Recorded Books
Books on Disk

I. Letter On Assistive Technology from The Administrator of The U.S Department of Education, Office of Special Education Programs

August 10, 1990

Dear Ms. Goodman:

This is in response to your recent letter to the Office of Special Education Programs (OSEP) concerning the obligations of public agencies under Part B of the Education of the Handicapped Act (EHA-B) to provide assistive technology to children with handicaps.

Specifically, your letter asks:

1. Can a school district presumptively deny assistive technology to a handicapped student?
2. Should the need for assistive technology be considered on an individual case-by-case basis in the development of the child's Individual Education Program?

In brief, it is impermissible under EHA-B for public agencies (including school districts) "to presumptively deny assistive technology" to a child with handicaps before a determination is made as to whether such technology is an element of a free appropriate public education (FAPE) for that child. Thus, consideration of a child's need for assistive technology must occur on a case-by-case basis in connection with development of a child's individualized education program (IEP).

We note that your inquiry does not define the term "assistive technology" and that the term is not used either in the EHA-B statute or regulations. The Technology Related Assistance for Individuals with Disabilities Act of 1988, P.L. 100-407, contains broad definitions of both the terms "assistive technology device" and "assistive technology service." See Section 3 of P.L. 100-407, codified as 29 U.S.C. 2201, 2202. Our response will use "assistive technology" to encompass "assistive technology services" and "assistive technology devices."

Under EHA-B state and local educational agencies have responsibility to ensure that eligible children with handicaps receive FAPE, which includes the provision of special education and related services without charge, in conformity with an IEP. 20 U.S.C. 1401(18); 34 CFR S.300.4(a) and (d). The term "special education" is defined as "specially designed instruction, at no cost to the parent, to meet the unique needs of a handicapped child" 34 CFR S.300.14(a). Further, "related services" is defined as including "transportation and such developmental, corrective, and other supportive services as are required to assist a handicapped child to benefit from special education." 34 CFR ss.330.13 (a).

The EHA-B regulation includes as examples 13 services that qualify as "related services" under EHA-B. See 34 CFR S.300.13 (b)(1)-(13). We emphasize that this list "is not exhaustive and may include other developmental, corrective, or other supportive services ... if they are required to assist a handicapped child to benefit from special education." 34 CFR S.300.13 and Comment. Thus, under EHA-B, "assistive technology" could qualify as "special education" or "related services."

A determination of what is an appropriate educational program for each child must be individualized and must be reflected in the content of each child's IEP. Each child's IEP must be developed at a meeting which includes parents and school officials. 34 CFR S300.343-300.344. Thus, if the participants on the IEP team determine that a child with handicaps requires assistive technology in order to receive FAPE, and designate such assistive technology as either special education or a related service, the child's IEP must include a specific statement of such services, including the nature and amount of such services. 34 CFR S.300.346(c); App. C to 34 CFR Part 3000 (Ques. 51).

EHA-B's least restrictive environment (LRE) provisions require each agency to ensure "(t)hat special classes, separate schooling or other removal of handicapped children from their regular educational environment occurs only when the nature or severity of the handicap is such that education in regular classes with the use of supplementary aids and services cannot be achieved satisfactorily." Part 121a, 42F.R. 42511.13 (August 23, 1977). Assistive technology can be a form of supplementary aid or service utilized to facilitate a child's education in a regular educational environment. Such supplementary aids and services, or modifications to the regular education program, must be included in a child's IEP. Id. Appendix C to 34 CF art 300 (Ques. 48).

In sum, a child's needs for assistive technology must be determined on a case-by-case basis and could be special education, related services, or supplementary aids and services for children with handicaps who are educated in regular classes. I hope the above information has been helpful; if we may provide further assistance, please let me know.

Sincerely,
Judy A. Schrag, Ed.D.
Director, Office of Special Education Programs

II. Individuals With Disabilities Education Law Report (Cite as 18 IDELR 627)

Digest of Inquiry

(Inquirer's Name Not Provided)
(Date Not Provided)

- Is a school district responsible to provide assistive technology devices for home use?
- May a school board overrule a determination by an IEP team that a child with a disability needs access to an assistive technology device at home?
- What is the time limit on implementation of an IEP?

Digest of Response

(November 27, 1991)

Assistive Technology Devices May Be Required for Home Use

If an IEP team determines that a child with a disability needs access to an assistive technology device at home as a matter of FAPE, then the school district must provide the device for home use in order to implement the child's IEP.

School Board May Not Change IEP Team's Determination

Under Part B, a school board has no authority to unilaterally change any statement of special education or related services contained in an IEP, including a statement of a child's need to have access to an assistive technology device at home. Without reconvening the IEP team, the school board may not change the IEP, and the school district is obligated to implement the IEP requirements, regardless of the school board's objections.

IEPs Must Generally Be Implemented

Under Reg. 300.342(b), an IEP must be in effect before the provision of special education or related services and must be implemented as soon as possible following the conclusion of the IEP meeting(s). In accordance with Appendix C to the Part 300 regulations, an IEP should generally be implemented without delay after being finalized, although a reasonable delay may be permissible in limited circumstances.

Text of Inquiry

I would like to have a copy of the policy classification on Assistive Technology.

I also have a question to ask regarding Assistive Technology such as a closed circuit TV.

My daughter uses a CCTV in school and it is on her IEP program. My daughter is visually impaired. The initial request was made by me, the parent, to the appropriate people involved in her education, and discussed and approved by the committee on an individual basis.

My question is: I would like to make the request to the appropriate officials for another CCTV for home use to accomplish the same results at home as is done in school. (For homework, reading books, any assignments from school).

Another question is: If the committee approves this request, it will go to School Board for approval. I would like to know what happens if the School Board doesn't approve the proposal? Is it impartial hearing time?

Thank you for your assistance in this matter.

Any information regarding Assistive Technology Informative for school and home use would be greatly appreciated.

Is there a time limit on implementation of yearly updated IEPs[?] Every year I have long delays on implementation of board approved IEPs[.]

Text of Response

This is in response to your recent letter to the Office of Special Education Programs (OSEP) requesting a copy of any OSEP policy clarifications on assistive technology, as well as asking specific questions concerning the assistive technology needs for your daughter. You also asked a question about the time limits for implementation of an individualized education program (IEP).

In response to your request, I am enclosing a copy of OSEP's August 10, 1990 letter to Ms. Susan Goodman concerning the obligations of public agencies under Part B of the Individuals with Disabilities Education Act (Part B), formerly cited as Part B of the Education of the Handicapped Act, to provide assistive technology to children with disabilities, along with some additional information on assistive technology and a copy of the Part B regulations. I would also like to provide you with OSEP's response to each of your specific questions as stated below.

I would like to make the request to the appropriate officials for another CCTV for home use to accomplish the same results as is done in school. (For homework, reading books, any assignment from school)

The IEP, which must be developed at a meeting that includes parents and school officials, must contain, among other things, a statement of the specific special education and related services to be provided to the child. See 34 CFR §§ 300.343-300.346. As stated in OSEP's letter to Ms. Goodman, if the IEP team determines that a child with disabilities requires assistive technology in order to receive a free appropriate public education (FAPE), and designates such assistive technology as either special education or a related service, the child's IEP must include a specific statement of such services, including the nature and amount of such services. See 34 CFR § 300.346(c); App. C to 34 CFR Part 300 (Ques. 51). The need for assistive technology is determined on a case-by-case basis, taking into consideration the unique need of each individual child. If the IEP team determines that a particular assistive technology item is required for home use in order for a particular child to be provided FAPE, the technology must be provided to implement the IEP.

If the committee approves this request, it will go to the School Board for approval. I would like to know what happens if the School Board doesn't approve the proposal? Is it impartial hearing time?

As part of the public agency's Part B obligation to provide FAPE to an eligible child with disabilities, the public agency must ensure that special education and related services are provided in conformity with an IEP which meets the requirements of 34 CFR §§ 300.340-300.349. One requirement, at 34 CFR § 300.343(a), is that the public agency conduct a meeting to develop, review and revise a child's IEP. The Regulations require that certain participants attend the IEP meeting. See 34 CFR § 300.344. The role of the participants at the IEP meeting is to determine the specific special education and related services that a child needs in order to receive FAPE. Once the determination is made at a meeting convened pursuant to 34 CFR § 300.343(a), Part B does not recognize any authority on the part of a local School Board to unilaterally change the statement of special education and related services contained in the IEP. After the IEP is developed and the placement decision is made by a group of persons knowledgeable about the child, the meaning of the evaluation data and placement options, the public agency must implement the IEP. See 34 CFR § 300.533(a)(3). Without reconvening the IEP meeting, the local school board could not change the IEP.

Is there a time limit on implementation of updated IEPs? Every year I have long delays on implementation of Board approved IEP's[.]

Part B imposes no specific time limits for the implementation of IEPs. The Part B regulations at 34 CFR § 300.342(b) require that an IEP: (1) must be in effect before special education and related services are provided to a child; and (2) must be implemented as soon as possible following the meetings required to develop, review or revise a child's IEP. The answer to Question 4 in Appendix C to the Part 300 regulations states that no delay is permissible between the time a child's IEP is finalized and when special education and related services is provided. It is expected that the special education and related services set out in the IEP will be provided by the agency beginning immediately after the IEP is finalized. In certain circumstances such as when the IEP meeting occurs during the summer or a vacation period, or where there are circumstances which require a short delay (e.g., working out transportation arrangements), the implementation may not be immediate. See Comment 34 CFR § 300.342.

I hope that this information is helpful to you. Please let us know if you have any additional questions or concerns.

Judy A. Schrag
Director
Office of Special Education Programs

III. Sample Letter Requesting an Assistive Technology Evaluation (Cite as 18 IDELR 628)

March 1997

Dear Sir:

Our daughter Catherine is currently receiving special education and supportive therapies through the public school district. As she is progressing through the elementary school grades, the curriculum is demanding more and more written work from her. At this point, teachers or assistants are writing for her, but this method does not allow Catherine the opportunity to compose written work on her own.

As Catherine's parents, we think the time has come to consider assistive technology for Catherine to allow her to learn to do written work on her own so that she can learn the mechanics of writing and can put her own thoughts down on paper for others to read.

To this end, we are requesting an assistive technology evaluation for Catherine to determine what kinds of technology are necessary to assist her with written expression. We are assuming that the assistive technology evaluation will be performed at district expense by professionals who are qualified to determine: (a) what assistive technology may be necessary for Catherine, (b) what assistive technology devices might be helpful, and (c) what occupational and physical therapy services may be necessary to support the technology.

We would like to have this evaluation completed so that information is available prior to the convening of the IEP Team to write Catherine's Individualized Education Program for next year.

We appreciate your assistance with this matter and look forward to hearing from you.

Yours truly,

IV. Assistive Technology ... Issues to Address

- What are the individual's current unmet needs for access to communication, writing, or educational materials?
- What are the short and long term educational goals?
- What are the daily educational demands which require the use of assistive technology?
- Have the appropriate team members, including parents, been involved in the assessment process?
- What are the features of the technology that would assist the individual in meeting daily classroom demands?
- Why is the selected equipment more appropriate than other alternatives?
- Have all of the individual's environments been considered?
- Does the selected equipment reflect the least restrictive intervention strategy?
- Is the equipment necessary to achieve educational/life goals?
- How will the individual physically manage the equipment in all environments?
- How will the equipment be integrated into the individual's daily life?
- How will the use of the assistive technology promote inclusion of the individual into activities in the school and community?
- Which members of the education team will be trained to use the equipment?
- How will the individual be trained to use the equipment?
- How will the family be involved with the individual and the equipment?

V. Educational Software Evaluation

A. IDENTIFYING INFORMATION

Name of instructional program _____

Publisher _____

Cost _____   Computer platform: PC   Mac

Other equipment needed to run program _____

Grade level of the program _____

Skill levels required of users _____

Special needs addressed by program _____

B.   DESCRIPTIVE INFORMATION

1. What is the purpose of the instructional program, as stated by its publisher?

_____

_____

2. What curriculum area or areas does it address?

_____

_____

3. What type of instructional program is it?

_____ tutorial drill and practice   _____ arcade game type

_____ drill and practice   _____ simulation

_____ problem solving   _____ educational game

_____ teacher utility   _____ other _____

4. For what type of learner was the program designed?

age level _____   grade level _____

ability level _____   interest level _____

5. What skills or information does the program attempt to teach or review?

_____

_____

6. How does the program present information?

__ text __ graphics __ animation __ color __ sound effects __ music

__ speech __ other _____

7. Is the information presented clearly?

_____ Is text legible and readable?

_____ Are graphics comprehensible?

_____ Are sounds audible and intelligible?

8. Are directions for using the program clearly stated and understandable?

Where do directions appear?

_____ within the program

_____ in the program's documentation or manual

9. Is the program under user control? That is, can the user:

_____ Control the program's movement from screen to screen?

_____ Review directions at any time?

_____ Exit the program at any time?

10. What computer use demands are placed on the learner?

_____ insert disk and turn on computer

_____ select from menu

_____ other _____

11. What academic demands are placed on the learner?

reading level _____

spelling level _____

other _____

12. What physical demands are placed on the learner?

_____ keyboard must be used to enter responses

_____ press any key

_____ press a key from one half or one quadrant of keyboard

_____ press on specific key

_____ press several keys in order

_____ other devices used to enter responses

13. What speed demands are placed on the learner?

_____ presentation speed controlled by program

_____ presentation speed under user control (moderate, fast, or slow)

_____ unlimited response time

_____ response time set by program (moderate, fast, slow)

_____ response time varied by user

14. What accuracy demands are placed on the learner?

_____ user can correct typing errors

_____ program does not allow correction of typing errors

_____ program locates common errors

_____ program requires correct spelling of all responses

_____ program allows only one correct response for most questions

15. Is feedback about response accuracy provided to learners appropriately?

_____ knowledge of results provided after each response

_____ correct responses confirmed

_____ learner informed if response is incorrect

_____ another trial provided if response is incorrect

_____ number of trials provided

_____ correct response demonstrated if learner fails to answer correctly

_____ opportunity to respond after demonstration of correct response

16. Does the program use any branching procedures besides differential treatment of correct and incorrect responses?

_____

17. What techniques are used for reinforcement and motivation?

_____ knowledge of results and confirmation of correct responses

_____ summary information about learner performance

_____ text message of praise for correct responses

_____ graphics display and or sound for correct responses

_____ competitive game in which correct response earns points

_____ other _____

Reinforcement is: _____ continuous _____ intermittent

18. What user options are available to students and teachers?

Students can select

_____ activity from menu difficulty

_____ number of questions, type of questions

_____ other _____

Teacher or parent can select

_____ sound on or off

_____ number of questions

_____ type of questions

_____ sequence of instruction

_____ number of trials

_____ speed of presentation

_____ speed demands for responses

_____ other_____

Teacher or parent can

_____ enter own content into program

_____ review student records

_____ other_____

19. Is the program's documentation adequate?

_____ All program features fully and clearly explained

_____ Rationale for program, purpose and objectives included

_____ Print materials provided for students

20. Other comments about the instructional program:

_____

_____

_____

C. OVERALL EVALUATION

Rate the appropriateness of the instructional program in each of the following areas, using this scale: 1=excellent, 2=adequate, 3=inadequate

1   2   3   Curricular content (program addresses important skills)

1   2   3   Interest level

1   2   3   Ease of use for learners

1   2   3   Demands on learner (e.g., computer use, academic)

1   2   3   Instructional procedures

1   2   3   Motivational value

1   2   3   Appropriate use of the medium

1   2   3   Important instructional variables under teacher control

1   2   3   Other _____

WHAT TO LOOK FOR:

Software Features
- Easy-to-Read Screens
- Consistency in Format
- Intuitive Characteristics
- Logical Labels
- Instructional Choices
- Graphics
- Friendly Documentation
- On-Screen Instructions
- Auditory Cues
- Visual Cues
- Built-in Access Methods
- Alternatives to a Mouse
- Optional Cursors
- Creation of Custom Programs

Alternative Input
- Switches and Switch Software
- Alternative Keyboards
- Keyboard Additions
- Access Utilities
- Interface Devices

- Voice Recognition
- Optical Character Recognition and Scanners
- Electronic Pointing Devices
- Pointing and Typing Aids
- Touch Screens
- Joysticks
- Trackballs
- Arm and Wrist Supports

Processing Aids
- Abbreviation Expansion and Macro Programs
- Word Prediction
- Talking and Large Print Word Processors
- Grammar and Spell Checkers
- Reading Comprehension Programs
- Writing Composition Programs
- Electronic Reference Tools
- Menu Management Programs

Alternative Output
- Braille Embossers and Translators
- Refreshable Braille Displays
- Speech Synthesizers
- Screen Readers
- Screen Enlargement Programs
- Monitor Additions

Specialized Products
- Closed Circuit Television (CCTV)
- Environmental Control Units (ECU)
- Notetakers
- Reading Machines
- Text Telephone (TDD)

VI. Assistive Technology Evaluation

Functional Analysis

Name: Chuck   **Date:** _____

Grade Level: Sixth

Overall Description: Chuck is a sixth grade student who receives all of his instruction in the regular classroom. Chuck has right hemiplegia. His right upper extremity is more affected than his lower extremity. He has difficulty with total body movements requiring bilateral coordination, especially with upper extremities. Chuck has a leg length discrepancy with his right leg being shorter than his left. He wears a lift in his shoe to compensate for the difference. Chuck has low average intelligence and normal speech. He reads at the third grade level, and does math at grade level, except for story problems. Chuck is very concrete in his thinking and has great difficulty understanding figurative language. Chuck has a full time aide in the regular classroom who modifies assignments and helps to keep him on task. Socially, Chuck is polite and well-behaved, but appears to be immature in his social relationships.

Need	Current Status	Next Step	Criteria for Success	Support Required	Locations
Cognitive Ability	Chuck is able to do grade level assignments, but he is very literal in his interpretations, especially of abstract concepts.		Completion of grade level assignments with evidence of understanding of main concepts.	Limit requirements to a few concrete concepts in each academic unit.	Home School Community Recreation
Attending	Chuck is very easily distracted both visually and auditorily.	Try having Chuck use earphones when he is word processing	On task 65-70% of time during independent work periods.	Distraction free environment; study carrel; proximity to teacher or aide.	Home School
Perception	Chuck has a blind spot which makes it difficult for him to track from line to line when he is reading. He also has trouble distinguishing figure from background.	Because of perception problems, Chuck must have a large display screen on his computer.	Complete modified assignments independently at least 85% of the time.	Enlarge worksheets and reading material. Highlight key vocabulary words. Use a cardboard window to isolate individual lines when reading. Enlarge on screen display when doing word processing.	Home School
Fine Motor: Hand Writing; Note Taking	Chuck can use only one hand for fine motor tasks, including typing. Chuck is an excellent one-handed typist both in terms of speed and accuracy. Chuck can write in cursive, but handwriting is very labor intensive and tiring for him. He produces much better written products using a computer. He cannot take notes and listen at the same time.	Try giving Chuck notes before the classroom presentation. Have him highlight keywords with a highlighting pen as he is listening to the discussion.	Able to produce written work at about the same pace as other students in his class.	Laptop computer; printer; enlarged screen display; Co-Writer with Write Out Loud for word processing and word prediction. Chuck needs to use word processing whenever written assignments are required. Whenever possible his written assignments should be shortened or he should be expected to respond using multiple choice or one word answers.	Home School Community Recreation
Self Help	Chuck cannot tie his own shoes and he has difficulty zipping his jacket with one hand.	Try having a peer buddy assist Chuck with his shoes and jacket.	Able to receive help with a minimum of fuss or embarrassment.	Teacher support of the peer buddy relationship.	Home School Community Recreation